PRAISE F

Real Happiness at Work

~~~~

"Gandhi said that work is also worship, but you would not know it from most meditation courses. There is meditation and yoga for stress, health, body perfection, or preparation for worship or spiritual life. But not much for that big chunk of time we call work—the elephant in our calendar. Here, Sharon Salzberg elegantly and articulately guides you to bring it all together in the workplace and in the place of work in our lives."

—LARRY BRILLIANT, MD, MPH, President and CEO,
Skoll Global Threats Fund

"Keep this book next to your computer or next to your bed—you'll be reaching for it regularly as you learn to become happier and more compassionate in the most challenging circumstances."

—MIRABAI BUSH, Senior Fellow, Center for
Contemplative Mind in Society

"Meditation teacher Sharon Salzberg brings to the workplace practical techniques and practices that will help workers in challenging jobs survive and even thrive. It is highly recommended for both workers and their supervisors."

—REVEREND DR. MARILYN SEWELL, Minister Emerita
of the First Unitarian Church, Portland, OR

"*Real Happiness at Work* represents the next revolution in achieving greater personal fulfillment at work. Sharon has captured the essence of compassionate workplace practices and how they can bring greater meaning and balance into our daily lives."

—PETER J. MISCOVICH, Managing Director,
Strategy + Innovation, Jones Lang LaSalle

"*Real Happiness at Work* is filled with insights and practical skills that can enhance your life, shift your perception, and create meaning in the work you do—all from the inside out. Her book offers the mindfulness tools necessary to help us navigate our work, manage our relationships, and develop a more emotionally sustainable life as a result."

—SEANE CORN, Cofounder, Off the Mat, Into the World

"In today's techno-saturated, always-on, 1,000-mph workplace, sometimes it feels like the world is moving too quickly for mindfulness. Sharon's book is perfect for those just starting out meditating, those looking to deepen their practice, and experienced meditators who need a reminder of how to apply the teachings in this most stress-inducing of settings. I wish I'd had it earlier—it would have spared me so much stress in office situations."

—MELISSA KIRSCH, author of *The Girls Guide to
Absolutely Everything*

"*Real Happiness at Work* offers simple and skillful advice that helps us to harness the challenges at work to cultivate happiness and promote well-being. May every worker and employer read this book! The world would be a better place!"

—RICHARD J. DAVIDSON, Founder and Chair, Center
for Investigating Health Minds University
of Wisconsin-Madison

"An astonishingly relevant and important book for this time, when nearly everyone struggles to do good work in a crazed climate of overwork, overwhelm, and exhaustion. As our task lists grow, often so does meaninglessness, thoughtlessness, fractured relationships, and cynicism. Sharon is a superb guide, offering practices that serve as a strong, trustworthy lifeline, lifting us from these drowning depths to rediscover how moment-to-moment presence offers us clarity, discernment, effectiveness, and joy."

—MARGARET J. WHEATLEY, author of
Leadership and the New Science

"As someone who works with extremely competitive people in a high-stakes, highly charged, and ego-driven environment, I found this book to be a lifeline to sanity. *Real Happiness at Work* is a personal field manual that teaches us that changes in the workplace begin as an inside job. By tapping into our inner-kindness, inner-compassion, and inner-joy, we can gently bring those qualities out in our fellow workers. Sharon lays out how a personal transformation can make you happier at work, and has the potential to infuse your entire workplace with a spirit of joy and cooperation that can enhance the creativity and problem solving needed to meet all the challenges of a twenty-first century workplace."

—TIM RYAN, U.S. Congressman and author of
A Mindful Nation

Real Happiness at Work

*Meditations for Accomplishment,
Achievement, and Peace*

Sharon Salzberg

WORKMAN PUBLISHING • NEW YORK

Library of Congress Cataloging-in-Publication Data is available.

ISBN 978-0-7611-6899-7

Design by Sarah Smith

Workman books are available at special discounts when purchased in
bulk for premiums and sales promotions as well as for fund-raising or
educational use. Special editions or book excerpts also can be created
to specification. For details, contact the Special Sales Director at the
address below, or send an email to specialmarkets@workman.com.

Workman Publishing Company, Inc.
225 Varick Street
New York, NY 10014-4381

workman.com

WORKMAN is a registered trademark of Workman Publishing Co., Inc.

Printed in the United States of America
First printing December 2013

10 9 8 7 6 5 4 3 2 1

ACKNOWLEDGMENTS

~~~~~

Books (or at least my books) seem to be born of a collective effort. For inspiration, exertion, encouragement, and clarity I'd like to thank Joy Harris, Bob Miller, Mark Matousek, Mary Ellen O'Neill, Ambika Cooper, and the many people who so openly told me their stories of work, whether full of happiness or not so much.

Mirabai Bush, Lesley Booker, Maia Duerr, Mudita Nisker, Dan Clurman, Ellen Carton, and Kristin Neff generously offered exercises and reflections that have been tested and refined through their own years of work helping people be clearer and happier.

Many years ago, Margaret Wheatley helped change the way I viewed organizations. I've been moved, too, by her latest work and the inclusion of the distress, even despair, many feel at work.

Diana Rose, cofounder of the Garrison Institute, with creativity and generosity, created and sustained a program bringing yoga and meditation to domestic violence shelter workers, which opened up my understanding of resilience (and enabled me to meet some really extraordinary women).

Books by Dan Goleman, Michael Carroll, and Chade-Meng Tan have greatly enhanced the application of mindfulness to the workplace.

My gratitude to the staff and members of New York Insight who created a forum for exploring issues of happiness at work, and Betty Rogers and the people who gathered in DC to help me continue that exploration.

Ai–jen Poo, director of the National Domestic Workers Alliance and the codirector of Caring Across Generations, is an inspiration. Her work is a reminder that respecting the dignity of all is the basis for a society to move forward in justice and in love.

And a nod to my own small meditation group, within which a variety of interesting and challenging jobs are represented. You all give new meaning to "Keep calm and carry on."

CONTENTS

~~~

Introduction

WHEN YOU TOOK THE JOB THAT YOU HAVE NOW, did you hope it would make you happy? Did you anticipate having a connection with your coworkers? How about the work itself? Did you imagine yours would be an occupation that would complement your life outside of work and mesh in a way that felt unique and rewarding?

If so, perhaps you've been surprised—or even disappointed. While some people are fortunate enough to love what they do for a living, the majority of people with jobs face challenges on a regular basis that undermine their ability to be happy at work.

Hannah is a thirty-two-year-old secretary at a consulting firm where competition, subterfuge, and resentment prevail. She describes the office as a place where "the loudest, most underhanded person wins."

Peter is a thirty-five-year-old social worker who enjoys helping people get healthy but feels increasingly burned out by the extent of his workload. He's having a difficult time separating himself from the pain of the people he's helping and is suffering from an escalating sense of helplessness and hopelessness.

Louise is a forty-year-old police officer who doesn't know how to separate herself from the aggression her job stirs up inside her. To get through her adrenaline-charged days, she tries to compartmentalize the anger and fear that come with the job, but then finds herself taking it out on her husband and children when she goes home.

Grappling with issues of work and happiness brings up many important questions: Is it possible—or even wise to try—to be happy at jobs we don't like? Can we really maintain our peace of mind in hectic environments filled with uncertainty? Can we find a skillful way to deal with times when we have tried hard to make a difference, yet feel ineffectual or exhausted? Might the quality of our leadership expand through restoring our own deeper happiness?

The answer to all of the above is yes. There are pragmatic tools at our disposal for becoming more productive, satisfied, and peaceful at work. I believe that foremost among these tools is the practice of meditation. For nearly forty years, I've taught techniques of concentration, mindfulness, and compassion meditations to thousands of people around the world. They have included groups of creative entrepreneurs, schoolteachers, police officers, artists, scientists, army chaplains and medics, doctors, nurses, firefighters, frontline workers in domestic violence shelters, as well as financial executives. People using meditation for greater happiness come from every walk of life, ethnic background, and belief tradition.

Through meditation, we can come to understand work problems as a potential source of achieving greater clarity, rather than as obstacles without redeeming value, and begin to recognize the true potential of the challenges that work brings our way. Although many people experience work as a burden, or worse, it is also a place where we can learn and grow and come to be much happier. In the words of teacher and former executive Michael Carroll, "Maybe problems arise at work not as interruptions or intrusions, but as invitations to gain real wisdom."

Adults who work full time spend more of their waking hours at work than anywhere else, and Americans spend more hours per year at work than citizens of any other nation in the world. It can be difficult to keep from confusing our core sense of ourselves with the role we play at work, but clarity about this is critical to our peace of mind.

How we approach work that's not always fascinating and manage our time and emotions to counterbalance stress and cope with disappointments is intrinsic to finding meaning in our work world. We discover that it is possible to be competitive without being cruel—and committed without being consumed. Even in a job climate where being fired is a real and present danger, we have the power to improve our work lives immeasurably through awareness, compassion, patience, and ingenuity.

As I listened to people's stories—students, friends, and researchers on the subject of work—a few common *un*happiness themes began to emerge: burnout and the need for greater resilience; time management and excessive hours or demands; questionable moral practices or challenges to personal integrity; feelings of losing a sense of purpose and the need for deeper, more durable meaning; condescension by superiors who do not listen and show a lack of compassion in decision making; boredom, distraction, and ineffectual multitasking due to a lack of concentration; the longing for creativity, surprise, variety, and a more open awareness fostering flexibility and change; and, finally, the desire to understand their work environment from a more open perspective.

These observations are about what is missing for so many, but they help clarify what is needed. They led me to consider the ideas that would begin to resolve those issues, and I identified what I think of as the eight pillars.

Each chapter in this book is named for one of these pillars and concludes with a series of meditations and exercises to try. The meditations are a pragmatic guide to a range of options—it is worth experimenting with them to see what you want to continue with. Even if you are reading a later chapter, you might wish to go back to earlier meditations to reexperience them on a deeper level. By the time you reach the end of the book, you will have an array of tools for cultivating greater stability, openness, and fulfillment while working.

The formal *meditations* will require ten to twenty minutes of your time; you might find it easiest to choose one or two and practice at home each day. The five Core Meditations found in the early chapters are mindfulness of the breath, identifying emotions, the body and walking, letting go of thoughts, and practicing loving-kindness. Together, these form a complete curriculum for establishing a meditation practice. The

THE EIGHT PILLARS OF HAPPINESS IN THE WORKPLACE

Balance: *the ability to differentiate between who you are and what your job is*

Concentration: *being able to focus without being swayed by distraction*

Compassion: *being aware of and sympathetic to the humanity of ourselves and others*

Resilience: *the ability to recover from defeat, frustration, or failure*

Communication and Connection: *understanding that everything we do and say can further connection or take away from it*

Integrity: *bringing your deepest ethical values to the workplace*

Meaning: *infusing the work you do with relevance for your own personal goals*

Open Awareness: *the ability to see the big picture and not be held back by self-imposed limitations*

other suggested meditations build upon the foundation of these five. Please feel free to experiment with them all, and see what you find most helpful or intriguing or challenging in a way that sparks your interest.

Once you feel confident with the meditations, you can incorporate them into your workday in the form of brief mini-meditations, as well as practicing them at home. The *exercises,* done either through reflecting or journaling, harness our creative thinking to refine the lessons learned through meditating and help us apply them to our work life. The *stealth meditations,* found throughout the book, specifically shape our ability to bring mindfulness, concentration, and compassion to our work.

As you explore and develop these eight pillars, may they serve to support you in your quest to establish a deep and abiding experience of real happiness at work.

CHAPTER 1

Balance

W E LIVE IN A COMPLICATED WORLD. The new normal of this overextended era requires us to juggle a growing number of demands. The massive influx of everyday content (as digital-agers call information) makes mindfulness a growing challenge, particularly in hectic job environments. As we ping-pong back and forth, between phone and computer, obligations and deadlines, we might well find ourselves longing for a modicum of balance to help us find equilibrium amid these multiplying distractions.

Balance is the first pillar of happiness in the workplace, because without it, it's hard to do a good job or enjoy our work. Without some breathing space in the face of constant demands, we won't be creative, competent, or cheerful. We won't get along well with others, take criticism without imploding, or control the level of our daily stress. Just as a solid building needs a foundation both level and strong, mindful balance provides the essential foundation we need if we want to weather the stresses of work and find a way to flourish.

THE STRESS FACTOR

According to several studies and surveys, a large majority of Americans consider work to be a significant source of stress in their lives, with more than half of those questioned indicating that they feel undervalued by their managers or colleagues and are planning to look for a new job in the coming year. According to a survey released in 2013 by the John Templeton Foundation, Americans are less likely to feel or express gratitude at work than anyplace else in their lives. Long work hours, lack of control over responsibilities, organizational constraints, interpersonal and task conflicts, role ambiguity, and fear of being fired along with chronic nervousness over the prospect of not getting hired elsewhere are among the most common stressors that make people unhappy.

David Rock, author of *Your Brain at Work,* has described in fascinating detail the intricate mechanics of the brain on creativity and stress. We know, for example, that self-described happy people have more new ideas. We now know that stress decreases our cognitive resources, whereas mindfulness induces what is called a *toward state* in the brain, an openness to possibilities. In this condition, we feel curious, open-minded, and interested in what we are doing—all excellent qualities for thriving on the job. Neuroscience tells us that creativity and engagement are essential to making people happier. But the technological onslaught of today's world can also become highly stressful. Long hours, hard work, and high pressure are exacerbated by our being permanently plugged in. Though the introduction of laptop computers, high-speed Internet, mobile technology, and social media have wonderful advantages in how we connect, they also reinforce behaviors that shut down the toward state and set us on autopilot.

One of my students, Sonia, recently gave up the freelance writer life she loved and took a job in a hectic office. With fewer magazines and newspapers hiring during the economic meltdown, she was forced to replace her quiet, self-reliant lifestyle with one in which she's overwhelmed on a daily basis by demanding colleagues and what she calls a fretful vibe. "Sometimes, when I'm in a meeting or working on a deadline, it occurs to me that I'm barely breathing," Sonia admits. "I'm surrounded by dozens of fast-talking, fast-moving, *breathless* people. My days are scheduled with meetings, brainstorming sessions, and conference calls. It's a little like panting all the time."

This is a common scenario. For many people, their working life becomes a kind of nemesis rather than a place where they feel happy and valued. The simple act of stepping over the occupational threshold—into the office, classroom, precinct, restaurant, hospital, shopping mall, factory, or wherever work begins—is to enter an environment filled with potential distress and uncertainty. Anxious about losing her job, Sonia feels as if she is losing *herself* in the process of making a living, and has no choice but to tolerate the consequences of her toxic environment.

Fortunately, meditation has the power to reverse the negative physical and emotional effects of stress. The act of training our attention so that we can be more aware of our inner thoughts, as well as what's going on around us in the present moment, primes our brain cells to fire together in patterns that strengthen the vital nervous system structures that are key in everyday tasks such as decision making, memory, and emotional flexibility, and nurtures qualities considered to be crucial components of happiness: resilience, equanimity, calm, and a sense of compassionate connection to others.

Stealth Meditation

Before beginning a new project or meeting or conversation, ask yourself, "What do I most want to see happen from this?"

"Emotions—and happiness in particular—should be thought of in the same way as a motor skill," says neuroscientist Dr. Richard Davidson, a pioneering researcher in the relationship between meditation and happiness. "Our emotions can be *trained*. Unfortunately, we don't take this revolutionary idea as seriously as we should."

Davidson explains that when stress overwhelms us, prompting us to become upset or do things we might later regret, it's a sign that our amygdala—the brain's trigger for the fight-or-flight response—has hijacked its executive centers in the prefrontal cortex. Our amygdala functions like an executive assistant or a speed-dial circuit, keeping an up-to-date record of anything that appears to be a threat to us. This primitive part of the brain makes us react in the same way every time the situation comes up, which means that we can sometimes behave in ways that are less than professional. That is why "the neural key to resilience lies in how quickly we can recover from that state," according to Davidson.

It is also why business schools have begun teaching mindfulness techniques to aspiring MBAs, and why mindfulness training has come to be recognized as an integral management skill by a growing number of mainstream corporations.

Mindfulness refines or clarifies our attention so that we can connect more fully and directly with whatever is happening. So many times our perception of what is happening is distorted by bias, habits, fears, or wishful thinking. Mindfulness helps us see through these, even if they do arise, and be much more clearly aware of what is actually going on.

I often use this example: Imagine you are on your way to a party when you run into a friend, who reports on his earlier meeting with your new colleague. He says, "That guy is so boring!" Once at the party, who do you find yourself stuck talking to but that new colleague. Because of your friend's comment—not even your own perception—you find yourself not really listening carefully or looking fully at him. More likely you are thinking about the next fifteen emails you need to send, or fretting as you gaze about the room and see so many people you'd rather be talking to.

But if you drop the haze that your friend's comment has induced, perhaps you'll discover for yourself, from your own direct experience, what you think of your new colleague. You can listen, observe, be open-minded and interested. By the end of the evening, you might decide that you concur and find him really boring. But perhaps not. Life provides many surprises when we pay attention. What's important is that we are not merely guided by what we've been told, by the beliefs of others, by dogma or prejudice or assumption, but that we shape our impressions by as clear and open a perception as possible.

Mindfulness is a relational quality, in that it does not depend on what is happening, but is about how we are relating to what is happening. That's why we say that mindfulness can go anywhere. We can be mindful of joy and sorrow, pleasure and pain, beautiful music and a screech. Mindfulness doesn't mean these all flatten out and become one big blob, without distinction or intensity or flavor or texture. Rather, it means that old, habitual ways of relating—perhaps holding on fiercely to pleasure, so that, ironically, we are actually enjoying it less; or resenting and pushing away pain, so that, sadly, we suffer a lot more; or not fully experiencing times that seem unexciting because we're oblivious to or take for granted the ordinary and the everyday—all these self-defeating, limiting reactions don't have to dominate.

We can easily misunderstand mindfulness and think of it as somewhat passive, complacent, even a little bit dull. I was teaching somewhere recently and began the formal meditation instruction, as I often do, with the suggestion to simply sit in a relaxed way and listen to the sounds in the room. Someone raised his hand right away and asked, "If I hear the sound of the smoke alarm, should I just sit here mindfully, knowing I'm hearing the smoke alarm go off, or should I get up and leave?" I responded, "If there's a fire, I'd 'mindfully' get up and leave!"

Stealth Meditation

As you sit down at your desk or work space, spend a few moments just listening to the sounds around you, and note your reactions to them.

I understood his question though. When we hear phrases commonly used to describe mindfulness like "just be with what is," "accept the present moment," "don't get lost in judgment," it can sound pretty inert. But the actual experience of mindfulness produces a vibrant, alive, open space where creative responses to situations have room to arise, precisely because we're not stuck in the well-worn, narrow grooves of our habitual reactions. In mindfulness, we don't lose discernment and intelligence. These qualities actually become more acute as stale preconceptions and automatic, rigid responses no longer continue to rule the day.

THE BEAUTY OF MENTAL SPACE

Meditation trains the mind the way physical exercise strengthens the body. Recognizing the benefits of teaching mindfulness and emotional intelligence in the workplace, major corporations are integrating these trainings into programs being offered to employees. They see that a centered employee creates a happier, more profitable workplace, just as a spacious, healthful working environment aids the well-being of their employees. Aware of this symbiosis, large corporations from General Mills to DuPont are investing significant time and effort in creative, cost-effective ways to ease stress so that they can recruit and retain the most valuable talent. These giant companies are leading the way in the business world toward embracing mindfulness and wellness as part of a work culture. Every building on the General Mills campus is equipped with a meditation room stocked with yoga mats and meditation cushions. "Compassion to ourselves, to everyone around us—our colleagues, customers—that's what the training of mindfulness is really about," says Janice Marturano, the executive who spearheaded mindfulness practice at General Mills, and who now directs the Institute for Mindful Leadership. "It's about training our minds to be more focused, to see with clarity, to have spaciousness for creativity, and to feel connected," helping employees to live a healthier, more productive, and peaceful life, making them less stressed workers and better leaders.

Meditation is proven to reduce the stress hormone cortisol and "everyone wants to lower their stress levels," as Mirabai Bush, cofounder of the Center for Contemplative Mind in Society likes to say. "It doesn't matter if it's a chemical company or a communications company, happy employees are more motivated and more loyal, and that makes for a better workplace." To demonstrate the efficacy of mindfulness on employee happiness, Dr. Richard Davidson teamed up with the CEO of a high-pressure biotech start-up and Jon Kabat-Zinn of the Center for Mindfulness, for an experiment. Their simple objective was to teach a group of employees how to focus completely on "whatever's happening in the present moment without reacting to it."

The results were striking: After thirty minutes of meditation a day for eight weeks, employees in the meditation group—in contrast to the control group—demonstrated a significant shift in activation of areas of the brain associated with positive feelings. Also, employees tended to remember what they loved about their work in the first place and had an increased ability to get in touch with that momentum again. Chade-Meng Tan, one of the principle designers of Google's "Search Inside Yourself" curriculum, has seen similar effects in his company's seven-week mindfulness program. "For a long time practitioners knew, but the science wasn't there," Meng, as he is known, says. "Now the science has caught up."

Some of us are affected by the environment we create. A museum's communications director named Gabriel described how he'd made his office a refuge. "Creating a calm environment is critical," Gabriel says. "And my colleagues really respond to it. My office is known as the place of calm and peace. I can close the door and meditate, sometimes before a meeting. Sometimes other people come and sit in my office when they need to chill out. It turns into a therapy room. People come in there to cry or to tell me what's going on. It makes me happy to provide this one spot that has a different energy. For myself as well as for colleagues."

EMOTIONAL INTELLIGENCE

When psychologist Dan Goleman popularized the notion of emotional intelligence (EI) twenty years ago, he helped redefine what "smart" means in our culture by moving from the old, exclusively IQ-based model to one inclusive of emotional life. We now understand that emotional and social intelligence can be just as important as IQ in determining well-being and success in the workplace. Emotions are contagious, biologically, and our ability to modulate mood and demeanor contribute to health or toxicity at work.

Emotional intelligence is divided into five primary aptitudes that can help us enormously at work. First, is *self-awareness*, the knowledge of our own internal states, preferences, resources, and intuitions. Before we can relate to others mindfully, we must be conscious of what makes us tick. Next, is *self-regulation*, which points to management of one's internal states, impulses, and resources. Additionally, there is *motivation*, learning how to gauge the emotional tendencies that habitually guide us toward our goals. This includes asking if we are doing things for the right reasons, for example, or overcompensating for insecurity. Another gift of emotional intelligence is *empathy*, awareness of other people's feelings, needs, and concerns. Finally, we cultivate *social skills*, and the ability to cooperate and induce desirable responses in others.

Merry Nasser, who works as a divorce lawyer and mediator, has seen emotional intelligence transform her experience of being with clients in highly stressful conditions. "Divorce cases are often extremely challenging because of the toxic emotions involved," Merry says.

"In a two- or three-hour mediation session, feelings of rage, contempt, and distrust surface, and it's sometimes difficult to get the parties to stop verbally attacking each other long enough to have a productive discussion. However, since I've been practicing meditation, it's gotten easier for me to understand that the bad behavior that I am witnessing comes out of the extreme pain that has brought the couples to this place. It's easier for me to feel empathy toward them, and to sit calmly and listen to their stories, which then enables me to respond with kindness instead of reacting with impatience or anger. Recently, after a particularly difficult mediation session on a complicated case, with both the clients and their attorneys present, the husband told me that he felt that I was the first person who had actually listened to him in his two-year-long contested divorce. And his feeling of being heard allowed him to be open enough to move toward a resolution of the case that had been elusive until that moment.

My meditation practice has increased my ability to bring some lightness and optimism to the painful and destructive process of divorce. I can show my clients that it's within their power to stop looking back at what has happened in the past, so that they can increase their capacity to move forward into a happier future."

Meditation leads to emotional balance, which in turn leads to equanimity. Author Melissa Kirsch has discovered that simple practice has profound results. "I will sometimes sit in a brainstorm meeting, exhausted and listless, and look around the room and silently offer loving-kindness to each person at the table, thinking: *May you be happy.*" She goes on to say, "A friend made that suggestion and it has helped so much. I've also found space for breathing in the busiest settings: in departure lounges, at my desk, and on the subway. Ten mindful breaths and I'm back in the moment again." A meditator I know, Iris Brilliant finds that optimizing the thirty minute break from her barista job can alter the rest of her day. "When I first got this job, I would use my breaks to check Facebook," Iris tells me. "Then I noticed that it didn't help me rest—it just made me more agitated and kind of distracted. Now I love to go outside in the sun if it's a nice day. This brings me into the present moment in a pleasant way. It helps me when dealing with intense, demanding customers. When I'm talking to people I perceive to be difficult, I take a moment to breathe and relax my body. It reminds me that there is no need to rush, and I can actually be present with the person. This makes the interaction go more smoothly."

The strategies apply to corporate leaders as well. Casey Sheahan, the CEO of Patagonia, is adamant about doing forty-five minutes of yoga and meditation every morning. "My practice begins with measured breathing and a focus on all the conflicts and frustrations that are bothering me," he says.

> ### *Stealth Meditation*
> Try to perform a simple, conscious act of kindness every day. It can be as simple as holding an elevator door, saying thank you in a sincere manner, or listening to someone with a clear and focused mind.

"Instead of ignoring them, I really look at them. If I am feeling stupid, angry, jealous, or humiliated, I bring total awareness and acknowledgment to those feelings. I admit my failures and own them. Then I usually start laughing as I realize how small and inconsequential I really am and also how ridiculous my problems are!"

When we bring deep awareness to whatever's bothering us, the same things might be happening, but we are able to relate to them differently. This is reinforced by Carl, a hedge fund manager: "Most of the immediate benefit I get during meditation is at work, as it's a very stressful, high-pressure environment with aggressive, frustrating personalities—myself included, some of the time. During the last month, I was in the middle of ongoing, exasperating debates with my boss, and it was easy for my blood to boil. I was dealing with it during the day, and at night I was stewing over it. My meditation helped a great deal. After meditation, my anger would melt into acceptance and a much more balanced and proportional reaction. What was a major issue earlier was suddenly something I had a totally different perspective on after meditating for thirty to sixty minutes. If I meditated before going to sleep, the quality of sleep was much better, and I experienced much less internal volatility the next day. It was a night-and-day change—it would only take a little bit of meditation to transform how I felt about a work conversation.

"The more I do it, the more it reinforces how the mind just spins stories. I can flip out at a conversation or smile and laugh off the exact same interaction. It just depends on whether I'm paying attention to my breath and what my thoughts are doing.

That was the other thing—on the days when my threshold for losing my composure was low, my body was tense and my breath was noticeably constricted. On days I meditated, my breath felt more open and relaxed, and so was my reaction."

TAKE A BREATH

Dr. Patricia Gerbarg, who has studied the relationship between stress and breath for decades, believes that we vastly underestimate the power of something as simple as our breath to settle the mind and body. "Most people don't realize that there is a reciprocal relationship between the breath and our emotions, and that improper breathing can create mental distress," Gerbarg states.

Sonia realized that her ability to recognize the connection between her breath and resilience allowed her to do something constructive before she reached a point of burnout. Frazzled by her chaotic, overcaffeinated office environment, Sonia knew she had to find a way to cope. She committed to returning to her meditation practice. The results have amazed her. "The first thing that I needed to remember was to *breathe*," she says. "One deep, meditative breath can settle my mind before a meeting or even just checking an email. It helps me accept what is happening, to listen and to observe what's going on without having to bark my opinion or change a situation."

Dr. Gerbarg recommends slowing the breath down to four to six breaths per minute at work in order to balance the body's stress response system. This leads to increased feelings of calmness, enhanced attention, clarity, and mental focus. This simple recommendation can be a beneficial way to break up an otherwise stressful workday, and it is an exercise in mindfulness that is easy to carry over into our downtime, too.

NEGATIVE EMOTIONS

Balance depends on the ability to work with negative emotions when they arise. Meditation teachers sometimes use the acronym RAIN—Recognition, Acceptance, Investigation, and Nonidentification—to describe how to deal with an emotion mindfully. As I wrote in my prior book *Real Happiness,* we tend to identify with our thoughts to an even greater extent than we do with our bodies. When we're feeling blue and thinking lots of sorrowful thoughts, we say to ourselves, *I am a sad person.* But if we bang our funny bone, we don't usually say to ourselves, *I am a sore elbow.* Most of the time, we think we are our thoughts. We forget, or have never noticed, that there's an aspect of our mind that's watching these thoughts arise and pass away. This is what we mean by becoming a witness.

According to Buddhist psychology, negative emotions fall into five general categories: *desire, aversion, sleepiness, restlessness,* and *doubt.* In the case of desire, wanting things or results isn't the problem; being grasping, clinging, rigid, and overattached to them is. Aversion can manifest as hatred, anger, fear, or impatience. Sleepiness is not just laziness, but also the numbing out, switching off, disconnecting, and sluggishness that comes with denial or feeling overwhelmed. Restlessness may show up as anxiety, worry, fretfulness, or agitation. And when it comes to doubt, we're not just talking about healthy questioning but rather the inability to make a decision or commitment. Doubt keeps us feeling stuck; we don't know what to do next. Doubt undermines wholehearted involvement in relationships and in our meditation practice, and robs us of having in-depth experiences at work as well.

As we practice witnessing, loosening the grip of over-identification (*This is who I am and who I always will be*), we see that these states are not the totality of our being, that they arise and pass away. This is an essential difference. We are reminded that our inner saboteurs, those mental voices that make us unhappy, are just visiting. They're not inherent to our being, forever and solid. They are born out of conditions; they come and go and are adventitious.

In describing our minds, I like to use the analogy of a visitor knocking at the door of your house. The thoughts and emotions don't live there. You can greet them, acknowledge them, exercise choice about how to relate to them, and watch them go. I can see myself at home, happily minding my own business, and hearing a knock at the door. I go to the door and it's an emotion like greed or jealousy. What might I do? In one scenario, I would fling open the door and say, "Welcome home, it's all yours!" I would immediately forget who actually lives here.

Without mindfulness, we find ourselves inviting these unwanted emotions into our minds, offering them succor and free reign. When we are busy at work, mindfulness slips away all the more easily. Negativity can inhabit our minds before we know it. Caught in its embrace, we become enmeshed and identified with it, then project these negative beliefs into an imagined, unchanging future. This can make difficult situations seem unbearable. *This boss will never change, and I will forever be his pawn. This salary will never go up; my colleagues will never like me; the work will never get less boring; I will die tethered to this measly desk.* You know the drill. We lose the sense of having choices and forget that things change. This is how negative mind states solidify and come to seem permanent.

Let's say a rush of intense anger overtakes you. Normally, we get lost in a repeated recitation of the provocation and become identified with the anger. *They did this, so I'm going to do that, and my vengeful act will destroy them!* That's one possibility. Another approach is self-condemnation. *I'm such a terrible person; I'm so awful; I can't believe that I'm still angry; I've been in therapy for ten years. How could I still be angry?*

But the third possibility, the way of balance, is first to say "Oh, it's anger. This is anger." If we can maintain that sort of balance, then we are able to take the anger apart and see into its nature. This decreases its power to take over our minds, something we may never before have appreciated since we were so busy reacting.

And what do we see? First of all, we see that anger is not just one thing. It is made up of moments of sadness, moments of fear, moments of helplessness, moments of frustration, and moments of panic. None of these sound good, and none of these feel good, but at least this is an accurate picture of an alive system. We are able to see anger's composite, conditioned nature, and that it's many things woven together that are all moving and changing. If we then take action based on our feeling angry, we will likely make better choices (and see more options) because we also acknowledge the complex of emotions within it.

With practice, we learn to respond more quickly to negative tendencies. Instead of catching ourselves fifteen regrettable actions later, we develop a visceral sensitivity to what's happening within us and curb our negative cycle right away. Mindfulness helps us to peel away the layers of reactivity within us. We have a tendency to pile on when it comes to self-judgment. Let's say we are afraid of something. Then we feel shame because of the fear. Then we feel anger in response to the shame. These add-ons become extra psychological weight and work to solidify our negative feelings. I am not suggesting that we talk ourselves out of our feelings; merely that it is skillful to remember their nature before we act on them. *Well, last time I exploded it didn't work that well. This might be a good time to leave the room and come back later.*

This leads to equanimity, the voice of wisdom that helps us accept what cannot be changed in the moment and learning to say, "Right now, this is it." Equanimity is not repression, denial, or evasion; it's a full-hearted moment of mindfulness and rest, reminding us that life fluctuates and so do we. The fear we are experiencing in the morning, for instance, may not be present in the afternoon. Equanimity leads to confidence that we can deal with whatever our experience is, which is critical to self-empowerment. We come to see that freedom is possible in the face of our demons. Then we have the strength to stare them down.

David, an executive assistant at a boutique public relations firm, experienced equanimity in action during one of his boss's frequent meltdowns. As the biggest fish in a diminutive tank, David's boss was hooked on power, which she exerted by biting her employees' heads off whenever a bad mood struck her. Her aggression made David's work life miserable till he took up the practice of meditation. "Sitting in meditation every day taught me that I'm much stronger than I thought I was," he says. "Learning to calmly observe my own mental tirades without running away—which is damned hard—taught me to have much less fear about my boss's emotional outbursts, and moments of high drama in general. During meditation practice, I saw how mental explosions happened and how quickly they passed if I didn't freak out and break my mindfulness. They were tempests in a teapot, really, when I stopped being so afraid of them. Now I do the same thing at work. I see my boss as a tantrum waiting to happen. I no longer live in fear of her tirades or take them personally. I know how quickly they pass. Now I sit at my desk and mind my own business. Sometimes I count my breaths to stay calm. This has changed my work life completely."

A bank manager named Stephanie also found her own sense of balance during a particularly difficult period of her professional life. She had worked for a bullying boss for a while, barely tolerating his abuse, till his anger boiled over and he attacked Stephanie in public. He insulted her by calling her foul names and throwing a stack of papers at her in front of the entire staff. After this, Stephanie had a choice. She could fight back and be fired, or leave. "Instead of retaliating, I decided to use the experience for my own benefit. I quit without giving notice—that was my only retaliation. Beyond that, I don't actually regret the experience because it made me realize that I can handle a lot and that I'm capable of dealing with a bully. Learning how to handle a person like that has helped me in the long run with all the personalities I've dealt with since. It taught me that I can deal with a really monstrous personality without stooping to his or her level and still get my job done."

TIME AND PRIORITIES

Time can seem to be our nemesis in the workplace. Often, there appears to be too little of it—when we're feeling overworked; or too much—when we're watching the clock, waiting for the workday to end. Mindfulness can help us to unhook from the stopwatch, even when the atmosphere is frantic, by returning us to the steadiness of our breath. Interrupting the stress cycle of pushing, rushing, and cramming, we come to see that our illusion of insufficient time is really just that: an illusion. While the clock-punching, scarcity model of "just so many hours in a day" keeps us pressured and diminished, a more relaxed, expansive approach to time reveals how much of this stress is self-induced. A fascinating study recently tested the illusory nature of time pressure among very busy people. Researchers from the Wharton School at the University of Pennsylvania, Harvard Business School, and the Yale School of Management, found that when overworked people volunteered their time to helping people in need, they reported feeling *less* pressured timewise than they had previously. In other words, "when a person volunteers his or her time, it makes them feel (paradoxically) more efficient, and therefore less stressed and hurried."

The practice of equanimity leads to improved time management. Mary Mudd, a project manager, has learned this to her delight. "I plan and think about the future a lot. It's part of the job," says Mary. "But it can also drive a person crazy. When I started meditating, I thought it would be impossible to do my job focused on 'now.' But I have learned that it's always good to focus on the present—whether that means giving all my attention to a project meeting or updating a project plan on the computer."

Many find that bringing qualities like mindfulness and equanimity into their work isn't actually the hardest part; the really hard part is even remembering that we want to, especially during times of turmoil or uncertainty or crazed, pressured momentum. Remembering is the key to bringing our values to life. Once we remember, we often find that we can access equanimity or mindfulness or compassion.

Some people are helped by establishing simple reminders: Mary now has "EQ" pasted to the keyboard of her computer to remind her of "equanimity" in the midst of aggressive timelines on her job. Joan sets her phone to ring a chime every half an hour so she can bring awareness back into the moment. Kathleen trains residents at the hospital "not to (mentally) bring the last patient into the next patient's room," so that they can actively listen to each patient. To do this, she instructs them to be mindful of the touch of the doorknob before they enter any room. For these reminders to be effective, frequency seems to be more important than duration, so it's a good idea to pick something that doesn't take all that long each time you do it, but that you'll do several times in the course of the workday.

Setting priorities is critical to maintaining balance and giving each task its proper attention. When determining whether or not a task is urgent, we can ask ourselves a few simple questions. Do I need to do this now? How many people are counting on this to do their jobs? What are the rewards of doing it now versus the detriments of putting it off? If you do need to multitask then it is wise to do so with nonurgent undertakings. Carrying on two important or urgent tasks simultaneously will not give either of them the full attention they require.

Stealth Meditation

If you start to feel overwhelmed, take a quick, centering moment—as short as following three breaths— to connect with a deeper sense of yourself.

An insidious belief exists in our culture that more is more: More pressure makes more creativity makes more production makes more money. Unfortunately, worker happiness doesn't usually figure into this equation. Though most of us like being busy at work, we do not respond well to being slammed with unreasonable demands or deadlines. Research shows a direct relationship between personal challenge and job satisfaction, and an inverse one between unhappiness and productivity. "People are happiest when they're appropriately challenged to achieve difficult but attainable goals," according to Harvard psychologist Dan Gilbert, author of *Stumbling on Happiness*. But a challenge and a threat are not the same thing. Bosses may be able to get employees to work by threatening them, for example, but they also create discontent in their workforce, a lack of loyalty, and the tendency for employees to do only as much as they absolutely have to. The antiquated paradigm of using punishment against employees as a means of controlling them leads to further unhappiness among workers stung by a lack of respect from superiors.

It's a mistake to place a higher value on boss-pleasing than on self-care. Martyrdom and overavailability do not make for a happy work life. When we prioritize emotional intelligence over behaving as if our needs don't matter, work becomes less conflictive. This can start by doing simple things to balance time pressure with mindfulness.

- *Take a lunch break.* You are most likely entitled to a thirty- or sixty-minute lunch break. This is your personal time to take a mental break from work and recharge for the afternoon, so take advantage of it.

- *Be realistic about your time.* You can't do fifteen hours of work in an eight-hour day.

- *Keep your personal life separate from your work life.* This will reduce stress and ensure that company business stays at the office and doesn't come home with you.

- *Understand your job description.* Don't feel you must always take responsibility for tasks that aren't yours. Of course, this does not mean you can't help a colleague in need.

BOUNDARIES

As clear as our intention may be to set healthy boundaries at work, speaking up for ourselves is not always easy. In competitive work environments where overachieving seems like a prerequisite to success, we may be confronted with a tough choice: allow others to trample over our boundaries for the sake of upward mobility, or stand firm and risk being passed over for promotions, raises, and accolades. We all have different parameters for what constitutes boundary violation. Some people are happy to be flexible when the payoff is important enough. Others require boundaries more writ in stone to feel comfortable with their scope of work.

It's important to be honest with ourselves about our own needs. Two examples will demonstrate how subjective and apposite boundary setting can be in different scenarios.

Liz recounts: "I was working as a waitress in a small upscale restaurant in New York City. The owner was also the head chef there. He was really quite difficult to work for. For the first few months, I had somehow escaped being yelled at by him, but I was waiting for my turn to come. One day, when I was feeling rather vulnerable, I made a mistake on an order and he lit into me. I'd like to say I had a pithy comeback and then walked out (as I'd always fantasized I would), but I just kind of took it, and retreated into myself, while the other waiters and waitresses looked at me in that horrible, pitiful way we all looked at each other when that happened to any of us.

"After that day, I resolved I would leave in a couple of weeks. The owner noticed the change in my behavior, as I was, of course, much less friendly after that day. His girlfriend asked me why my behavior had changed. I was honest and said I was upset by the way the owner yelled at me that day and felt it was unjustified. He went on to argue, believing he was completely in the right. I disagreed with him but remained calm, as I was resolved that I was leaving. I finally said I thought he was abusive and that I didn't want to work there anymore. I then got my things together and left, saying good-bye to the other staff there. In the end, I felt good that I had been able to look him in the eye—even though I still found him intimidating—and calmly say I felt he was abusive, rather than yelling and storming out."

Mark's attitude toward boundaries at work was entirely different. At twenty-eight, Mark is a fledgling artist willing to do almost anything to advance his career as a painter. When a friend recommended him for a gofer job in the studio of a respected artist, Mark didn't hesitate. "I have an MFA, a great portfolio, and I'm scrubbing floors in somebody else's studio," Mark says. "I never thought I'd be happy doing somebody's laundry or being called to work on Sunday morning to buy cat food," he says with a laugh. "But the truth is that I'm loving it. I learn something new every day, just from watching how he works. I'm making no money, but know that this is right for me. When it stops being right, I'll move on down the road. Till then, I'm happy."

In mindfulness practice, wise discernment is a tool that can help us in boundary setting. Mindfulness may open the doors of perception, but it does not deprive us of critical judgment. Meditation and other mindfulness practices help us see *what is* more clearly, including what doesn't work for us. Increased awareness enables us to discern whether a particular experience we are having is one that we want to put more energy into, or one that we want to stand back from and allow to fade away. Mindfulness helps us to set boundaries by revealing what makes us unhappy and what brings us peace. It also helps us hone the ability to prioritize our tasks at work, and balance the demands of the job with the requirements of our own well-being. Mindfulness helps us to focus, increases our efficiency, strengthens our balance, and dissolves conflict and frustration arising from lack of clarity.

A CULTURE OF WELLNESS

A program I have been involved with at the Garrison Institute offers mindfulness training through meditation and yoga to domestic violence shelter personnel, hoping to reinforce resilience skills in the face of the incredibly stressful environment in which they work. Every day their jobs bring to light how horribly people can betray one another, brutalize one another. Every day their jobs reveal just how close a person can come to giving up all hope.

We began the project with frontline workers—the ones who dealt directly with the women and tried to help them construct a path out of their situations—then after some time included managers, directors, and supervisors. Our commitment was to train more than just one person from each shelter so they could be supportive of one another throughout the program and beyond.

To start, we would come together and list what stressors we faced at work. Then everyone would write a list of their usual coping strategies. Those who chose to would read those strategies out loud. Listening to music was probably the single most common tool people mentioned, though of course the kind of music varied wildly. Some people said getting out into nature helped, but this was not an easy thing for many since most of the shelters were in highly urban areas.

One woman said, "I watch a lot of *American Idol*." I really laughed at that one, since, as I disclosed to the group, the one time I had watched the show I got quite tense. It felt to me like watching constant rejection. Clearly not all methods of seeking repose work for everyone!

Some people listed behaviors they were using to deal with stress that they wanted to replace, like drinking. We were there, after all, to experiment with new tools of mindful awareness, to see what kinds of benefits they might bring.

After some time, as they explored the meditation practices and began enjoying less stress and more balance, participants looked at the possibility of a changed collective experience, and began talking about "creating a culture of wellness" at work. The participants recognized that if they could stay connected to the truth of their own worth, support and nurture it, a greater balance and more happiness at work could be achieved. Because of that balance, they could sustain their remarkable service instead of feeling overwhelmed. One woman spoke of replacing the junk food they brought in regularly with healthier snacks. A group determined that they would start a rooftop garden. Several spoke of starting meetings with a few minutes of silent reflection. Everyone spoke of creating some kind of tranquil spot—a quiet corner, a meditation space.

Stealth Meditation

Unitask! Focus exclusively on just one thing for a small portion of time. Try setting a timer for 15 minutes, so you can focus without straying.

No matter how big or small a space you see as your domain—a domestic violence shelter, an office, a classroom, a cubicle, or your own mind and body—if you set out to create a culture of wellness, you will come to know far greater balance. Out of that foundation of balance, considerable happiness can emerge.

✦ CORE MEDITATION: Breathing

This classic meditation can deepen concentration by teaching us to focus on the "in breath" and the "out breath." Sit comfortably on a cushion or chair and keep your back upright, without straining or overarching. If you can't sit, then lie on your back on a yoga mat or folded blanket with your arms at your sides. Just be at ease and close your eyes, or gaze gently a few feet in front of you and aim for a state of alert relaxation. Take three or four deep breaths, feeling the air as it enters your nostrils, fills your chest and abdomen, and flows out again. Then let your breathing settle into a natural rhythm, and just feel the breath as it happens, without trying to change it or improve it—all you have to do is feel it. Notice where you sense your breath most intensely. Perhaps it's at the nostrils, or at the chest or abdomen. Then rest your attention as lightly as a butterfly rests on a flower—only on that area—and become aware of the sensations there. For example, if you're focusing on the breath at the nostrils, you may experience tingling, vibration, or pulsing, or you may observe that the breath is cooler when it comes in and warmer when it goes out. If you're focusing on the breath at the abdomen, you may feel movement, pressure, stretching, or release. You don't need to name these feelings—simply let your attention rest on them, one breath at a time. (Notice how often the word *rest* comes up in this instruction. This is a very restful practice). You don't need to make the inhalation deeper or longer or different from the way it is. Just be aware of it, one breath at a time.

Whenever you notice your attention has wandered and your mind has jumped to the past or the future, to judgment or speculation, don't worry about it. Seeing your attention has wandered is the signal to gently let go of whatever has distracted you and return your attention to the feeling of the breath. If you have to let go over and over again, that's fine—being able to more gracefully start over when we've become distracted or disconnected is one of the biggest benefits of meditation practice.

~~~~~~

MEDITATION: Balance

Two of the forces that we're cultivating in meditation practice that will foster greater happiness at work are tranquility and energy. Sometimes these are described as calmness and alertness, relaxation and investigation. In any method of meditation we work to bring these together, to bring them into balance. So it's said that from the beginning this is reflected in our posture. For those of us who work at desks, this meditation can be done seated in your chair, but try not to focus on your computer. If you can, keep it out of your line of sight, or put up a picture of something calming, like a flower, or just close your eyes. Sit with your back straight without being stiff or tense. Don't use too much energy. You also don't want to lean against the back of the chair or be slumped over so that you're likely to fall asleep. You want to be upright, calm, and relaxed. Close your eyes or keep them open and center your attention on the feeling of the normal, natural breath. And notice the play of energy or interest and calmness or relaxation, and how you are with the breath. Are you a little disengaged and don't care really what it feels like? Focus a bit more, feel the actual sensations at the nostrils, at the chest, or at the abdomen. Do you have sort of a death grip on the breath, thinking: *If I hold on really tight, my mind won't wander?* In fact, your mind will wander more if you're tense, so loosen up a bit. If you can feel yourself balanced with calmness and alertness, you'll see how just one breath is tremendously fulfilling. We're not overriding it, we're not shrinking back from it, rather we're meeting it completely.

Sometimes in my own practice, I use this image of holding something in my hands that's very fragile, very precious, like something made of delicate, fragile glass. If I were to grab it too tightly it would shatter, but if I were to get lazy or negligent and my hand fell open, the glass would fall and break. So I just cradle it, I'm in touch with it, I cherish it. That can be a metaphor for your breath. You don't want to grab it too tightly or be too loose, too energized or too relaxed. We meet this moment and we meet this breath, and we cherish it, one breath at a time.

If you find yourself feeling too far back and disinterested, come forward. If you're too far forward, too tense, trying too hard, then settle back. Let the breath come to you. If you feel you should be adjusting the balance, don't worry about it. You needn't question yourself, *Am I too tight? Am I too loose?* Let your intuition arise, then come back to the place in the middle. It's just one breath.

If you have too little energy, you'll get sleepy, sluggish, dull. If you feel that way, sit up a little straighter. If your eyes have been closed, open them, maybe take a few deep breaths to allow the sensation to be more intense, and then once again allow the breath to become natural. Aim your attention toward just one breath, it's the whole universe, nothing else matters.

If you have too much energy you'll feel restless, agitated, worried. If that happens, see if you can feel the sensations of one breath, as though your hands were in water and you felt the water swirling around, all the different sensations. So, too, with your mind, your attention, you can feel the sensations that will soothe you and ground the energy. You can feel just one breath. And with it feel the sense of balance.

And when you feel ready, you can open your eyes and reengage with the world around you.

~~~~~~

CORE MEDITATION: Emotions

The practice of mental labeling, which means naming the feeling or thought that's arising in the present moment, serves two main purposes: First, it establishes a sphere of awareness, a small, calm interior space where we aren't caught up in a thought or feeling, aren't reacting to it, but are able to discern it, name it, and move on. Second, noting provides a kind of instant feedback system: We can see whether we're labeling our experiences with openhearted acceptance (*yep, this is what's happening right now*) or with fretfulness and resentment (*oh, no; not envy again!*). If we hear that tone of judgment or self-criticism, we can let it go and say to ourselves again, more kindly and evenly, *ah, there's envy*. Try to make the noting a warm, open acknowledgment. Noting performs a third interesting function: It reminds us vividly and efficiently of the way things continually change. Many thoughts and emotions will come, be noted, and go during the course of our workday, some of them very pleasant, some upsetting, some neutral. They arise; they subside. Our job is simply to note them without judgment, to see the truth of this very moment, and then breathe.

In this meditation, the state of awareness we're going for is balanced and gentle, but also alert and awake and connected to what's going on around us. Think of how you feel when you're taking a walk in nature, or chopping vegetables for a great meal.

Take a comfortable posture, sitting or lying down, and close your eyes or lower your gaze. Settle into awareness of your body. Be aware of sounds, and then turn your attention to the breath. Be aware of any feeling strong enough to take your attention away from your breath and make it the object of your meditation. Name it, using mental noting if you like. Usually it works best to note the existence of an emotion two or three times to know it is more than fleeting (e.g., happiness, happiness; disappointment, disappointment; boredom, boredom). And so on. If no emotions arise that are strong enough to distract you, just keep following your breath. Listen to the tone of your mental noting. Here's one way to tell whether you're doing that: If it's harsh or tense: Jealousy, jealousy! Again! Then make an effort to note more gently: Jealousy—I know you. I know how you operate. Forgive me if I chose to ignore you just now . . . " Another useful approach: When you've located the emotion in your body, for example, if you find that anxiety has created a knot in your stomach, check the rest of your body to see whether some other part is tensing up. Consciously relaxing that reactive tension will help you more calmly observe the knot of tension in your stomach, allowing it to begin to relax on its own. The very act of observation can sometimes dissipate stress, because we're not struggling against the experience but taking an interest in whatever feeling arrives and passes away. If you find you're adding on judgment, condemnation, or projection into the future (*I'm crazy to feel this way*), remind yourself that it's okay to be feeling whatever has come up. Try letting go of those reactions as best you can, and coming back to your direct experience. After a few moments, open your eyes. Later, see if you can tune into your emotional landscape and notice the variety of your feelings throughout the day.

~~~~~~~~~

MEDITATION: Drinking Tea

In this meditation, we try to be more fully present with every component of a single activity. At a time when you're not likely to be distracted or disturbed by obligations, make yourself some tea. Fill the tea kettle slowly, listening to the changing tone of the water as the level rises, the bubbling as it boils, the hissing of steam, the whistle of the pot. Slowly measure loose tea into a strainer, place it in the pot, and inhale the fragrant vapor as it steeps. Feel the heft of the pot and the smooth receptivity of the cup. Continue the meditation as you reach for a cup: Observe its color and shape and the way it changes with the color of the tea. Put your hands around it and feel its warmth. As you lift it, feel the gentle exertion in your hand and forearm. Hear the tea faintly slosh as you lift the cup. Inhale the scented steam and experience the smoothness of the cup on your lips, the light mist on your face, the warmth or slight scald of the first sip on your tongue. Taste the tea; what flavor do you detect? Notice any leaf bits on your tongue, the sensation of swallowing, the warmth traveling the length of your throat. Feel your breath against the cup creating a tiny cloud of steam. Feel yourself put the cup down. Focus on each separate step in the drinking of tea.

Q&A

Q   **What does it mean to be mindful in the workplace?**

A   To be mindful is to be more aware, in the moment, of our experience; to be more present and more open. Though we might fear this state of mind would hinder our ability to get things done, the opposite is true. To return to focus from reverie, to cultivate the ability to begin again after an error, to have a way to not be so lost in anxiety and misinterpretation, to be able to listen deeply—these are all aspects of mindfulness, and they can all enhance the creativity, refinement, and production of our work. Also, people who are mindful are often the ones who laugh more often and more easily.

Q   **Can we benefit from meditation practices if we limit them to small pockets of time during the day, such as the commute to and from work?**

A   Yes, we do benefit from small pockets of practice. One of my Tibetan meditation teachers counseled, "Short moments many times," as a way to make progress in meditation. What I find personally though, is that if I have a period of time dedicated specifically to meditation, say ten to twenty minutes in the morning, I am much more likely to remember to be aware of my breath or my emotions when commuting or periodically throughout the day during different activities.

Q **How would I specifically use the tool of mindfulness to deal with irritation toward a colleague?**

A It often helps to pay attention to the feeling of irritation—not so much the story of why you're irritated, but the actual feeling of it. What does irritation feel like in your body? Where do you sense it? How does it feel as a mood? This doesn't mean you will never take constructive action or set clearer boundaries or whatever is involved in the irritation, but it helps tremendously to be able to identify irritation as it's starting, rather than after you've taken regrettable action. With a more immediate recognition of what we're feeling, we have a choice as to how we want to respond in that moment.

CHAPTER 2

Concentration

C ONCENTRATION STEADIES AND FOCUSES our attention so that we can let go of unhealthy inner distractions—punishing regrets about the past, manufactured worries about the future, addictive tendencies—and keep from being seduced by outer ones. Distraction wastes our energy; concentration restores it.

We often experience our attention as scattered. We sit down to think something through or work through a dilemma, and before we know it, we're someplace else. Maybe we're lost in thoughts of the past, often having to do with something we now regret. *I should have said that more skillfully. I should have been less timid and spoken up. I should have been wiser and shut up.* We aren't thinking about things in order to find a means to make amends or act more responsibly; instead, we're stuck in what is past.

For some of us, distraction can propel us into anxious thoughts of the future. For someone who might be an anxious flyer, facing a flight and all the timing issues that come with it can be stressful—especially without the power of concentration. Imagine the mind of a worried flyer sitting on an airplane at a busy airport. Suddenly he starts thinking, *Oh no, I think this plane might leave late. I'm sure it will be late. Now I'm going to miss my connection. That means I'm going to arrive in Portland, Oregon, after midnight. There won't be any cabs! What's going to happen to me? I'll never make it to my hotel, and I won't make my meeting the next day! I'll lose my job,* and so on.

When I see my own mind beginning that arc of anxiety, I have a saying I use to help restore me to balance. "Something will happen." *Perhaps there will be a bus. Or I'll spend the night in the airport. Something will happen. I can't figure it all out right now.* Without concentration our minds just spin off into the future, in a way that isn't like skillful planning, but is more like exhausting rumination. Concentration is the art of gathering all that energy, that stormy, scattered attention, and settling with it. It doesn't mean we never think about the past or the future; it means we're not so subject to anxious speculation, to self-sabotaging patterns of thought, to deferring a sense of possibility to some far-off day, instead of seizing it today.

> **Stealth Meditation**
>
> If you are on a conference call, refrain from checking your email or doing another task at the same time.

One friend of mine, a very busy executive, was an endless ruminator at work, always in his head and one step out of sync with the department he controlled. This disjunction caused a lot of grief among employees who accused him, sometimes to his face, of being unfeeling, callous, and distant. My friend is none of these things. He's just a worrywart who has a very hard time staying in the present moment. He has trouble concentrating because, as he says, "My mind is going one hundred miles an hour trying to stop bad things from happening." Although it is often the welfare of his department, and, by extension, those who work there, that keep him distracted, the real-life human beings around him accuse him of being "a suit" who doesn't care about them. One day, an intern with nothing to lose told him that he was rude and obnoxious. "She said, 'Earth to whoever you are, I'm talking to you,'" he remembers, "and it snapped me out of my trance. I was a million miles away. She busted me, and I'm grateful she did."

Most of us have our own versions of being absent or distracted, that we use as occasional (or habitual) shields at work. These fuzzy mind states create barriers we might not be aware of and weaken connections and job performance in general. Concentration bolsters mindfulness, on the other hand, and in turn is strengthened by mindfulness, because we can let go of distractions more and more easily as we grow more mindful. Turbulent thoughts, futile regrets, anxious wanderings may arise, but they arise accompanied by less and less "glue." Then they don't take hold of our attention and spin us away from the home base of the present moment.

ATTENTION

When it comes to work, cultivating the ability to steady our attention and concentrate on the task at hand can lead to greater satisfaction. "Mindfulness has to do with paying attention to what's happening in the moment without judgment," says Mirabai Bush, "Sometimes people think being mindful means being slow. It's not about being slow, it's about being slow enough that you can pay attention to things. It requires a certain intelligence to be able to focus on many things at the same time." Besides making us more productive, strength of attention is directly related to *subjective well-being,* a term used by positive psychologists to describe personal levels of happiness. Mind wandering on the job has been shown to dramatically decrease happiness in the workplace, in fact, and concentration increases the good feelings that come with immersion and flow. Feeling good about what we do for a living depends more on our moment-to-moment experiences than it does on prestige, status, or pay. Being present is its own reward and offers benefits of both empowerment and integration. Think about all of the energy we waste as we are caught in the past, in the future, in judgment and speculation. Then imagine capturing all of that energy, so that it is returned to us, a force we can gain access to, utilize, and shape. That's a source of tremendous power. And we don't need to beg, borrow, or steal that energy, chemically induce it or inflate it—it is ours, allied with our attention and ready to be redeemed.

Concentration also integrates the different parts of our experience into a cohesive whole. The larger manifestation of distractedness is often a feeling of fragmentation. This is the way we can have so much compartmentalization and role identification in our lives—not because it is always useful, but because we are accustomed to inner division and evasion, reacting in the moment without much of a sense of a core or center to our lives. It is due to this pattern that people often say, "I feel like I'm one person at work and a completely different person at home." So much of the day we feel disconnected from parts of ourselves, let alone from others. As we develop more concentration, the different threads of our experience are seamlessly woven together, and we discover an essential sense of who we are and what we care about. Then we can lose the way we often have of setting ourselves apart from the moment and come fully alive as we engage in our tasks, no part left out, as my absentminded friend learned when his intern called him on his rudeness.

Meditation helps us stay on task longer and be less distracted by our environment, which in turn lowers our stress level. While *one-pointed attention* may appear to slow us down, the practice of limiting ourselves to one activity at a time frees our mind of distraction and actually makes us *more* productive.

Rita Arens, deputy editor of a national women's website and business called BlogHer, learned this after years of feeling crazed at work. "I get several hundred emails a day at two different accounts," Rita says. "I need to keep up with Twitter and Facebook as well as find time to work on my personal writing projects—my blog, my novel—and be the wife and mother I want to be. 'Overwhelmed' is my mood most days. The multitude of distractions used to affect my ability to concentrate, which left me feeling strung out and anxious." Rita's meditation practice has helped to strengthen her ability to focus when barraged simultaneously with multiple demands. She has learned that while it's unrealistic to try to stop the number and variety of incoming demands, in our technologically advanced world it is possible to modulate how much information we're taking in, and how many tasks we are doing at once. When we slow down and concentrate on doing just what is before us to be done now, we become the masters of our own environment rather than its frantic slaves. Through concentration, we're able to narrow the scope of our attention and choose what we need to focus on. "It's not always possible to remove myself from situations, but it is always possible to stay with my breath for even just a minute." The practice of one-pointed attention has helped to decrease Rita's stress and transformed her working life by strengthening her concentration.

A whole new form of attention deficit disorder has emerged from the overwhelming atmosphere of the modern workplace. Attention deficit trait (ADT) is workplace-induced attention deficit caused by the constant, relentless input of

Stealth Meditation

Pay attention to your hands. See if you can make the switch from the more conceptual thought of "these are my fingers," to the world of direct sensations—pulsing, throbbing, pressure. You don't have to name these sensations, just feel them.

information, these days usually enabled by our high-tech devices, smartphones, and computers. Unlike attention deficit disorder (ADD), people aren't born with ADT. According to Edward Hallowell, the psychiatrist who identified ADT, its symptoms are widespread and appear to describe most people who have jobs—at least some of the time. He identifies the symptoms of ADT this way: "When people find that they're not working to their full potential; when they know that they could be producing more but in fact they're producing less; when they know they're smarter than their output shows; when they start answering questions in ways that are more superficial, more hurried than they usually would; when their reservoir of new ideas starts to run dry; when they find themselves working ever longer hours and sleeping less, exercising less, spending free time with friends less, and in general putting in more hours but getting less production overall."

Never in history has the human brain been asked to track so many data points. As working people today struggle to keep up with the onslaught of information streaming toward them in the digital age, poor job performance caused by multitasking has become a major problem for employers as well as for employees. The reason for this is that, contrary to popular belief: *Human beings seem to be cognitively unable to multitask.* Multitasking is a modern myth that contributes to low self-esteem at work, fraying our nerves, and harming our job skills as we struggle, and fail, to master a skill for which the human brain is unprepared.

MULTITASKING

We would like to believe that attention is infinite, but it isn't. That is why multitasking is a misnomer. The brain can focus only on one thing at a time. We take in information sequentially. When we attempt to focus on multiple tasks simultaneously, what actually happens is that we switch back and forth between tasks, paying less attention to both. This does not mean that we can't walk and chew gum at the same time, of course. What we cannot do is concentrate in the same moment on two distinct, input-rich activities that require our attention. While we may be able to talk on the phone and stir coffee simultaneously, we can't carry on a conversation and text at the same time without losing information and time. Studies show that when people are interrupted and have to switch their attention back and forth, they take—on average—50 percent longer to accomplish the task and make up to 50 percent more errors. That's because each time you switch tasks, your brain has to run through a complex process to disengage the neurons involved in one task and activate the neurons needed for the other. The more you switch back and forth, the more time you waste and the lower your quality of work.

Strung out by information overload, however, many of us are becoming habituated and addicted to distraction. "Successful" multitasking has been shown to activate the reward circuit in the brain by increasing dopamine levels— the brain chemical responsible for feelings of happiness. The danger of this is that the dopamine rush feels so good that we don't notice we're making more mistakes. This is comparable to the rush you might feel while playing the slot machines in a casino. Stimulated and entertained by the flashing lights, the ringing bells, and the distracting, carnival-like atmosphere, gamblers go into a pleasure trance, addicted to the illusion of winning money when, in fact, they're going broke.

Stealth Meditation

Every time you feel bored, pay more acute attention to the moment. Are you listening carefully or are you multitasking? Try to be fully present with just one thing.

It's important to be aware of how multitasking can stimulate us into mindlessness, giving the illusion of productivity while stealing our focus and harming performance. "When you are walking, walk. When you are sitting, sit," is ancient wisdom. Hopping rapidly from one thing to the next, answering the phone while we're shuffling papers while we're sipping a latte, we fritter away our attention and forget more easily. In addition to dopamine, multitasking prompts the release of adrenaline and other stress hormones, which contribute to short-term memory loss as well as long-term health problems. This also means that the information we take in while multitasking is harder to retrieve later than information we take in while concentrating. That is why learning to be a unitasker in a multitasking world is so vital.

Rather than divide our attention, it is far more effective to take frequent breaks between intervals of sustained, one-pointed attention. A Web designer named Brian figured this out for himself with no knowledge of neuroscience. "I work for a community news site and have to be online from nine to five," Brian says. "It can really fry the brain and get tedious. I've found that if I take ten minutes or so for every hour of work to do something for myself, like read somebody's blog or take a walk, it helps me concentrate when I turn back to my duties." Although this may sound difficult, Brian's increased focus enables him to return to the task at hand with surprising ease. "Instead of hopping from thing to thing—which is so tempting with the Internet—I focus on what's in front of me. Then I let myself dillydally to give my brain a rest. When it comes to work, less is definitely more in terms of feeling satisfied. And efficient." While this may sound counterintuitive, relaxing our focus for regular intervals and pacing our sustained concentration sharpens attention and renders the mind more flexible.

Debunking the myth of multitasking, we become much better at what we do and increase the chance of being able to remember the details of work we have done in the past.

BOREDOM

Boredom is a common nemesis at work. Boredom does not necessarily arise from having too little to do, however. Feelings of boredom arise from disengagement regardless of the cause. From frontline service workers to corporate executives, workplace boredom is rampant for two primary reasons. First, a difficulty in finding *meaning* in the work we do; second, the absence of *variety* in our daily tasks. Uninterrupted routine and perceived monotony are great challengers of concentration. While today's employees may be busier than ever, many are not tremendously inspired. In a tough economy where it's riskier to change jobs, employees may stay in the same place so long that they feel stuck and uncreative.

Of course, everyone (even people who love their work) is bound to be bored at work sometimes. That's why some employers in high-risk occupations are installing built-in countermeasures to fight boredom on the job. The Transportation Safety Administration, for example, rotates its officers to different tasks every half hour in order to keep them from getting bored, and help keep them sharply focused. "We want eagle eyes at each of those posts," a TSA officer explains. "We like to say there's never a dull day at TSA."

Interesting as such ideas can be, each of us, anytime we want to, can dispel boredom through attention. The wonderful thing about mindfulness, as many meditators know, is its power to make the most ordinary things interesting. The more closely we attend to experience, the more fascinating its details become. Fritz Perls, one of those who brought Gestalt therapy to the United States, said, "If you are bored, you are not paying attention." Understanding this, boredom becomes a valuable feedback tool for us, telling us not that the situation or person we face is too confining or wearying, or somehow lacking but rather that our attention at that time is halfhearted.

When we do pay full and wholehearted attention, we can't help but notice that no two moments are ever alike, however monotonous they may appear to a distracted mind. The same job at the same desk reveals itself to be wholly different, one day to the next, when we're fully engaged in experience moment by moment. The next time you're struggling with a project but unable to focus, rather than spinning your mental wheels, I suggest that you give yourself a time out. Take a ten-minute walk, preferably outdoors, to relax your weary mind. This is a good alternative to Brian's habit of Web-surfing. Going a step further and turning it into a walking meditation would be ideal for relaxing your resistance to the task at hand. I will talk more about this in the chapter on resilience. Using skillful means to befriend our overworked minds, instead of persecuting them to distraction, returns us to equanimity and the ability to focus.

PROCRASTINATION

The ancient Greeks had a word that lies at the heart of procrastination: *akrasia,* which means doing something against our own better judgment. When we procrastinate, we act against our own self-interests, satisfying the desire for immediate gratification by sacrificing our own longer-term goals and well-being. The essence of procrastination is to willingly defer something even though you expect the delay to make you worse off. The pile of important papers you never quite get to. The new job you put off looking for even though going to your current place of employment is the bane of your existence. Whenever we knowingly delay doing what's necessary in favor of the easier, less important task, we feed the demon of procrastination.

Haven't you noticed how much harder it can be to make positive changes—and break bad habits—than it is to slack off and stay stuck? We can endlessly anticipate difficulty and failure; uncertainty of outcomes alone is enough to keep us from taking action. Many people suffer from perfectionism and fall into the "If I never finish, I can never be judged" syndrome. Others use procrastination as a way of avoiding disappointment and performance anxiety. They may tell themselves in the moment that they are opting for the more pleasurable thing by avoiding what they don't want to do, but procrastination lowers subjective well-being, rather than the other way around.

A psychologist named Joseph Ferrari has isolated five justifications that we use to explain procrastination and justify the behavior. First, people who procrastinate overestimate the time they have left to finish tasks. This is part of what is called "the planning fallacy." Next, they tend to underestimate the time that it actually takes to complete said tasks. Third, they overestimate how motivated they're likely to feel the next day. For me, though, the fourth and fifth reasons are the most interesting. The fourth one is that procrastinators tell themselves that succeeding at a task requires that they feel like doing it; and, fifth, is entertaining the false idea that working when not in the mood is somehow suboptimal—that it's best to wait till the lightning of inspiration strikes before motivating ourselves to stop procrastinating.

Doreen, a visual artist, lives in a perpetual state of severe postponement. Her apartment is an obstacle course of unfinished work, half-folded clothes strewn around the house, the kitchen sink half-filled with dishes—piles of evidence all around, testifying to Doreen's inability to force herself to do things she doesn't enjoy even though they need to be done. Since Doreen works from a home studio and is self-employed, she lacks the benefit of a structured job, which only exacerbates her problem. Chronic procrastination leaves her feeling depressed, angry with herself, and only a fraction of how successful she might be if she got her act together.

When asked about her procrastination, Doreen talks about feeling powerless in her own life—"unequal" is the word she uses. She feels she has too many things to do and too little time with which to do them. Not knowing where to start, she dithers, unable to prioritize or take action. "The thoughts in my head are like pea soup," Doreen says in an exhausted voice. "Everything just runs together." To counteract her anxiety about putting things off, Doreen spends a minimum of three hours a day on her bed watching TV and avoiding the tasks she hates herself for avoiding. "It seems like a vicious cycle, like there's a cog missing somewhere inside me." She means a cog in her motivating engine. "I stall when I should be working. I can't figure out how to get a grip on the next thing to do. It makes trying to work at home just impossible."

I offered Doreen a challenge. For thirty days, she agreed to approach one task a day—and one task only—from Monday till Friday. If a task took her longer than a day to complete, she was instructed to maintain this single focus until the task was completed (regardless of how many days this took). When she caught herself obsessing about her litany of uncompleted tasks, Doreen's practice was to draw her attention back to the present moment and simply do *just the next thing*. When tempted to stop halfway and start something else, I instructed her to use reality checks to slow down. "First I'll finish the copy. When the copy is done, I'll write the email," and so on. Though skeptical of any success, Doreen agreed to this thirty-day experiment in focusing.

A month later, Doreen's actions had changed dramatically. When she came back to me, she seemed amazed by what had transpired. "When my mind settled on just the next thing, I could feel my whole body relax," she said. "When I finished the first thing—organizing my desk—I felt like I was standing in balance for the first time in as long as I can remember." One by one, Doreen completed tasks in her home office with increasing speed and facility. "I learned that I could focus this way. One by one. Just that closet. Just that mailing." After the experiment in "just the next thing" was complete, Doreen claimed to feel better about her prospects as a visual artist, and generally to like herself more.

Technology like email, Facebook, and Twitter are catnip for procrastinators, of course. Attending to a trivial email or being distracted by minutiae can give us an instant hit of gratification or accomplishment, what psychologists call a "quick win," while keeping us from real work. This leads to feelings of guilt; but guilt is not a solution. The most effective practice for countering procrastination is to identify our problem areas—business letters, networking, whatever it might be—and take small steps in a methodical way toward those tasks we tend to put off. By breaking large projects into small, easier to complete steps, we make them more palatable, focusing our minds on just the next thing, one piece at a time.

Focused, wholehearted, stable attention is a capacity we can cultivate, of course. When we meditate, training our minds in focus, we are practicing a transferable skill. We are also cultivating the art of concentration at work. The focus that is developed through following our breath is the focus that will help us pay full attention to the task—the letter, the email, the conversation—we must complete before surfing the Web or taking a break.

Business Insider program director Arden Pennell is a dedicated meditator and says, "It's tough, particularly in this office, because the quality of mind that Business Insider is asking you to cultivate is to be constantly watching what's happening and to be reading all the news feeds, all the time. I get distracted, too, but one of the things that meditation teaches is muscle memory, repetition. You sit on the cushion so many times, your body and nervous system start to learn the practice, noticing when you're distracted, and dropping it, taking a breath and coming back. And so, if you've done that so many times, it becomes easier to access even in the flow of life. So it's training, like going to the gym. It trains the brain to notice when you're getting distracted. Meditation creates more decision space around everyday tasks."

CORE MEDITATION: Walking

Walking meditation is literally a step-by-step way to bring mindfulness into everyday activity. To begin: Let your attention rest fully on the sensation of your feet and legs as you lift them and place them on the ground. Be sure you have enough space to walk at least twenty steps, at which point you'll turn around and retrace your path. Start by standing comfortably at the beginning of your chosen path with your feet shoulder width apart and your weight evenly distributed. Hold your arms at your sides in whatever way seems comfortable and natural. Become aware of your foot making contact with your shoes, if you're wearing them, and then with the ground; note what you are feeling. Slowly shift your weight onto your left foot. Notice the way your muscles stretch, strain, and relax and any cracking or popping in your ankles or trembling in the weight-bearing leg. Carefully move back to the center, then shift onto your right foot and leg noticing what your body feels as you make this adjustment. Gently come back to center and stand for a moment. Be aware of the sights and sounds around you without getting lost in them. If you're outside, you may find yourself distracted. That's okay. When you notice that your mind is wandering, bring your attention back to the stepping. The very moment you recognize that you've been distracted, you've begun again to be aware. Finish one step completely before you lift the other foot. Check in with the sensations in your legs, hips, back—any pressure, stiffness, or fluidity. Then come back to the sensations in your feet and legs. Newcomers may feel a bit wobbly, and the more slowly you move and the more aware you become, the more unbalanced you might feel. If that happens, speed up a bit. Do the same if your mind starts wandering or you're having trouble connecting with your bodily sensations. Experiment with pace until you find the speed that best allows you to keep your attention on the feeling of walking and that lets you remain most mindful. After twenty minutes or so, simply stop and stand. Notice what you feel at the point where your feet meet the floor or ground; take in what you see and hear around you. Gently end the meditation.

If walking is a problem for you, you can do this meditation without literally walking. Instead, sit (or lie down if that's best) and focus your awareness on another part of the body—moving your hand up and down, say—or on the sensations of wheeling if you're in a wheelchair. When the instructions call for slow, deliberate, focused movements of the legs and feet, do the same with whatever part of the body you're using.

Once you have experimented with this in dedicated chunks, try it in transitions such as getting to work, going from room to room at work, all at a normal pace.

~~~~~~~

CORE MEDITATION: Letting Go of Thoughts

This is a good meditation to practice at the workplace, in between meetings or tasks.

- Find a comfortable place to sit and resolve to concentrate on your thought process for five minutes. Let your mind appear as a blank screen and watch carefully for thoughts to arise. They may come as images or words in the mind or both together. Some thoughts may arise with a feeling or tactile quality as well, such as shoulders tensing or butterflies in your stomach. Make note of your experience, writing it down if you wish.

· For five minutes experiment with counting your thoughts. After noticing and counting the thought, simply wait, looking at the blank screen for the next one to arise. Remember, some thoughts are very subtle, like *It's so quiet in here.* We count the thoughts not to form a judgment about ourselves and how much or how little we think, but to observe the thought process with mindfulness, without getting lost in each story. Thoughts arise and pass away outside of our will or wishes. What we're experimenting with here is not adding associations, interpretations, and judgments to our thoughts, in other words, not thinking about our thinking, simply observing.

· Carefully note each breath as "breath." As thoughts arise, note them simply as "not-breath." This also helps us cut our dualistic fixation with the content of our thoughts; whether lovely or frightening, they are all noted simply as "not-breath."

· What kinds of thoughts predominate in your mind—words, pictures, those arising with a kinesthetic (physical) sense, or a combination?

· If images are arising, can you note them as "seeing" and notice if they are growing brighter, fading, breaking apart, moving closer, or staying just the same?

- Can you note the particular kind of thought, such as "planning," "remembering," "judging," "loving"?

- Observe the effect of various types of thoughts, such as a future thought like *I'm never going to get any better.* What happens to your mood, to your body as a consequence of this thought? What is the difference between simply observing it and getting lost in it? Remember the metaphor of greeting emotions as visitors at the door.

- Think about one of your insistent thoughts and see if you can give it a label that reflects some compassion and humor. Insistent thoughts might be called the top-ten tapes because they arise as conditioned "recordings" in the mind. They play like songs on the radio, reflecting the same themes over and over again. Try labels like the "Martyr track," the "I Blew It Again track," the "Fear of the Dark track," the "Great World Teacher track." Be lighthearted with these labels. We can see these recordings as conditioned forces and don't have to take ourselves so seriously. The repeated forces in the mind can be greeted in a friendly and openhearted way. "Oh, it's you again. The Mad Scientist recording. Hello."

- If a particular thought seems to be returning a lot, notice whatever emotional state may be feeding it. Unseen feelings are part of what brings thoughts back again and again. For example, anxiety often fuels future planning. At first the emotions may be half hidden or unconscious, but if you pay careful attention, the feelings will reveal themselves. Use the sensations in your body to help guide the attention to whatever emotions may be present, For example, being conscious of tension in the chest may uncover sadness. Begin to note whatever emotions you feel as a way of acknowledging them.

• If there is a repeated physical pain or difficult mood, pay attention to the thoughts, stories, or beliefs that may be feeding the difficult situation. When we are mindful, we may find a subtle level of self-judgment or a belief about our unworthiness, such as *I'm not as good as others. I'll always be this way.* These thoughts actually help perpetuate the pain or unhappiness. Once we see the distinction between our actual experience and the thoughts we add to it, we can relinquish those unhelpful add-ons and return to our direct experience.

~~~~~~~~

EXERCISE: Awareness of the Body

Here's an anchoring exercise you can use if your mind is wandering and you feel disconnected from yourself in this moment. It's simply focusing on your body's touch points. If you are busy and engaged in several activities at once, and following your breath isn't helping anchor your attention, become aware of your body's touch points—the small areas, about the size of a quarter, where your back, thighs, knees, or buttocks are in contact with the chair or cushion, your hand is in contact with your knee, your lips are touching, your ankles are crossed. Focus on these points of contact; picture them, feel them. Doing so may pull you away from your spiraling thoughts and bring you back to this moment.

Q & A

Q How do I learn not to multitask so much?

A When we began the Insight Meditation Society, a witty friend created a mock brochure for us. In the brochure he gave us a made-up motto, "It's better to do nothing than to waste your time." I think of that in terms of multitasking. You can experiment with specific tasks, making a point of fully doing one thing only. On a particular conference call, resolve not to read email at the same time. At a meeting, practice deep listening, instead of mentally planning the next day's meetings. And take short breaks throughout the day, even just a few breaths' worth, where you do nothing. It feels as though that will make for a crushing overload of things left undone, but in fact we are a lot more productive that way than in time-wasting multitasking.

Q Would you provide a "micro-meditation" that I can quickly do at my desk before a big presentation or meeting?

A   I would suggest a one- to three-minute version of settling your attention on the feeling of the breath, the actual physical sensations of your inhalation and exhalation. This will cut through the momentum of feeling rushed and overburdened. Or, if you wish, do one simple activity without multitasking—drink a cup of coffee, get up and stretch, walk down the hall. Your mind will wander, but for that one- to three-minute period you don't have to try to do more than just that one thing.

Q   **If meditation tells us to slow down and notice what's happening, how do we incorporate that message into a workplace where speed is valued, whether it's a quick response to a question or a fast turnaround on a project?**

A   If you are working in a very fast-paced environment, see if you can build in some periodic respite to help you center and come back into the present—one minute before a meeting to simply breathe, a brief pause before sending an email, or getting outside for a short break. Then you will feel refreshed and connected to the moment as you move quickly through the next period of work, without being so overcome by momentum that you lose touch with yourself. One benefit of a fast-paced society is that 60 seconds can feel like a luxury when you spend it on yourself, and it is not likely to adversely affect your production during a busy day.

Q How might I deal with irritability toward someone at work when I'm trying to concentrate on the task at hand?

A You might see if you can put the irritable feelings aside, for now, and deal with the present moment's needs. It's not that irritability is a bad thing to feel; you're just making the choice to pay attention to something else for a while. Acknowledge your thoughts and feelings, and in effect put them on a shelf, saying "not right now." This doesn't mean that you never seek resolution of the situation you find irritating. It means you will do so at a time and place of your choosing, instead of being driven by the irritability into distraction or hasty action. Meditation practice fosters that choice, by helping us develop our "letting-go muscle," our ability to not be so caught in everything that comes up in our minds.

CHAPTER 3

Compassion

COMPASSION CAN RADICALLY IMPROVE our day-to-day work lives. Even if we work alone, the practice of compassion and loving-kindness toward ourselves and others is an essential pillar of on-the-job happiness, shifting the emphasis from *me* to *we*. Compassion is the recognition that conscious or unconscious unhappiness is the cause of so many difficult behaviors, and loving-kindness is the wish that all beings be peaceful and happy. When we bring these qualities to work with us, and remember to keep our hearts open even in challenging situations, we promote not only our own well-being, but the happiness of our colleagues as well.

This can be a challenge, of course. Competition, conflict, job pressure, stress, and a host of other professional ailments, often conspire against the desire to practice loving-kindness. Instead of wishing one another peace, we may feel inclined to dwell repeatedly on criticism or blame, refusing to give others the benefit of the doubt. When we close our hearts to the people we work with, we create suffering internally and externally, spewing ill feeling into the workplace and isolating ourselves behind a wall of disinterest.

JUDGMENT

Marion dreads her lunch hours with her colleague Kate. Backbiting, aggressive, perpetually miserable, and prone to tirades of gossip and mischief, Kate insists on inviting Marion to lunch every couple of weeks to air her many grievances. Marion clenches her teeth through these unwanted lunch hours, feeling like she's trapped on a boat with her least favorite person.

Kate has her own challenges. Wracked with fibromyalgia, married to a heavy drinker, she struggles to keep her emotional balance in a professional setting where she is deeply unpopular. Instead of opening her heart to her vulnerability, Kate channels her pain through defensiveness, alienating the people she talks to, starting with Marion. "I know that I should feel sorry for her," Marion admits. "But she's just too mean. I can't feel any compassion for her." Marion struggles to tolerate Kate while being painfully aware of her own emotional limitations. "I can't get past my own judgment. And the judgment is the real problem." Marion admits that Kate embodies qualities she finds close to intolerable. Even when Kate attempts to open up personally, Marion's heart stays closed.

Harsh negative judgment is a major obstacle to happiness in the workplace. Since empathy is the prime inhibitor of human cruelty, as Dan Goleman, the author of *Emotional Intelligence,* says, it's important to notice where judgment blocks us from appreciating the suffering of others. In order to be part of a team effort, we must learn to move from me to we, which is possible only when we challenge our assumptions about other people, recognize our common bonds, and prioritize the tasks at hand over our personal ego. As comedian Margaret Cho says, "Try to love someone who you want to hate, because they are just like you, somewhere inside, in a way you may never expect, in a way that resounds so deeply within you that you cannot believe it."

This can be enormously difficult, of course. But it is possible. Tom's experience is a good case in point.

"Several years ago, I was given six weeks' notice to finish a project and leave a job that was really important to me. I felt 'scapegoated,' furious, and compelled to clear my name. Strong emotions flooded my body and mind. The idea of going to work the next morning felt toxic. But I cared a lot about the project, so abandoning the work was not an option.

"I consulted my meditation teacher who said, 'You will not be able to right this wrong.' I needed to practice compassion, for my employer as well as myself, in order to diffuse the anger. Resentment cannot thrive in the presence of the love and concern you develop in compassion practice, so I began to practice for the well-being of all the people I worked with, for my supervisor in particular. This is what's called 'giving merit' to others with the fruits of our meditation practice.

"Almost immediately, I noticed changes within *me*. Instead of being bound with rage, I felt liberated, almost relieved. These feelings motivated me to engage with my work with renewed creativity. Things were going more smoothly, and even my supervisor commented on how I seemed different. At the end of the six-week period, I was asked to stay on the project, but I chose to leave out of compassion for myself. I knew that there were problems there I couldn't fix, so I had to go."

To be with others openly, to share a workload with good humor and a generous heart, is one of life's most uplifting experiences. The essence of teamwork is selflessness and generosity, which is why work can be a powerful spiritual practice. At work, rigid judgment often arises from insecurity, fear, and envy. With competitiveness comes a judgmental edge. It may be adversity toward a professional rival, the one who's getting what should be yours. Such categorization often arises from the false belief that the other person's success and your misery are somehow a permanent, unvarying, inflexible state. What makes joy for others tough is our assumption that there isn't enough good stuff to go around, and the more someone else has, the less there will be for us. Sometimes we are in direct competition of course—we've applied for the same promotion, or the same grant, and if you get it, I don't. Quite a lot of the time, it isn't like that, but we feel inside as though it is.

At times we witness someone else's success or good fortune and we feel that the accolade, the prize, the praise was heading right toward us, but it got rerouted somehow to another person instead—as though something has been stolen from us, and we feel bereft. In the moment when we're feeling envy or resentment, if we observe our habitual reaction, we notice the suffering it creates. When we cultivate happiness in our own life, we will be able to take pleasure in the happiness of others. Joy for others depends on a feeling of inner abundance and the knowledge that our lives are worth something. Loving-kindness meditation helps us tap into that knowledge.

Andrew, a filmmaker, currently working as a digital media coordinator, describes this very well: "I love the movies. I love everything about them, and I believe in them. I believe they have the power to sneak into people's perceptions and change them, to incite questions, to shed light on neglected topics and people, to confront the emotional experience of being human, and to transmit wisdom.

"When I realized how competitive the industry is, and to a certain extent, how much of a game it is, my reaction was predictably cynical and pessimistic. The odds seemed so stacked that it wasn't even a question of hope—it was a test of will. I became very guarded against fellow filmmakers, judging them and comparing their abilities and potential to my own. I would get angry when I would hear about other young filmmakers getting awards, or receiving recognition. I would be angry with myself for not working harder to be more disciplined and productive. And this would turn into sorrow and shame at my obsession with others' good fortune, at my focus on the end and not on the journey, my neglect of my own experience and work and story.

"In this regard, the lessons and power of loving-kindness take on a particular relevance. During a meditation session, I realized that I am grateful for the competition. I am genuinely happy for all of those working and striving for the same expressive end, for those whose work bears the mark of their sincere devotion to and fascination with depicting humanity in all its flawed beauty and detail.

"Instead of being afraid of the number of people seeking to make films, I am inspired to think of how many other inquiring minds I will surely meet in my quest. And being grateful instead of threatened has opened my mind to my own potential and brought me back to my original and pure love for filmmaking and storytelling, sans trivial worries and ambitions."

LOVING-KINDNESS

I was once teaching a class and a woman raised her hand. She said, "I feel filled with loving-kindness and compassion for all beings everywhere . . . as long as I'm alone. Once I'm with others, it's very rough." We all laughed, because we all knew what she meant. It isn't easy taking an interest in people whom we hardly know. It isn't easy maintaining an open mind toward people we dislike. It can seem thoroughly counterintuitive that these efforts might make us happier, but there are few practices that have more profound and liberating effects on our day-to-day lives.

I discovered this many years ago when I was first learning loving-kindness meditation in Burma, now sometimes known as Myanmar. One of the preliminary exercises was to look for the good in someone—even someone you didn't like. The idea isn't to help delude us into thinking there are no problems, or to encourage us to withdraw into conflict avoidance. But if all we think about, day after day, over and over again, is someone's faults, we will build an ever more solid wall of alienation between us. If we can find just one good thing about someone and reflect on it, our view of that person broadens, and we are reminded of the complexity and challenges we all face in life. We still see all the problems, but we also feel a different quality of connection to the person we are contemplating.

It is common to believe that people are fixed, solid entities instead of ever-changing creatures with shifting desires, fears, and a range of possible behaviors. This realization relies on emotional intelligence and will yield many benefits—we see people differently, we listen to them more carefully.

Sometimes, finding one good attribute in someone is not going to happen—because of our hurt or repugnance or history, that exercise is unrealistic. In that case we do a different reflection, which is a consideration that everyone wants to be happy. Everyone wants to feel a sense of belonging, of being at home in this life, somewhere, even those people who seem to proclaim the opposite. Out of confusion and ignorance, we might choose actions that lead us far from that goal. So many of us know a person who complains of loneliness, only to drive well-meaning people away with an ill-temper and unreasonable demands. But the bottom line is that we all want to be happy. Even *that* person.

Another instruction I got in Burma that I initially found quite odd was, "If you are annoyed at someone, give them a gift." *What in the world is that about?* I thought, *How bizarre!*

The practice isn't meant to be a bribe or to promote denial of a wrong, but serves to break open a dynamic of resentment or hostility and allows us to see what happens without that filter of certainty we have when we think, *You're a pain!* I tried it, and it was so interesting. I left a treat outside someone's door, so that she didn't even know it was an offering from me. I saw her open her door, spot the treat, and the most beautiful childlike smile broke over her face. *Oh,* I thought. *She's a lot more human than I had projected her to be. May she be happy.* One funny repercussion of this advice—every once in a while someone gives me a surprise gift, someone who would certainly also know that teaching, and I find myself wondering if I've annoyed them in some way!

The point of all these practices is to help us take some risks with how we pay attention, and break free of the fixedness with which we tend to view ourselves and view the world around us.

Mirabai Bush uses an exercise in her mindfulness training that includes having workers stand across from each other while the leader of the exercise says certain phrases. The leader will say, "Just like me, this person has suffered in life. Just like me, they've made mistakes and have regrets. Just like me, they want to be happy." She says, "It cultivates an appreciation of that person as someone trying to do the right thing, even if their behavior hasn't been to your liking. It gives you an understanding that like you, they have desires and they also have insecurities. People do things that can hurt you and most of the time in the workplace, it's not personal."

COMPASSION IS A FORCE

We do not always view compassion and loving-kindness as the strengths they are. They are often viewed as secondary virtues—at best—in our competitive culture: If you can't be brave or brilliant or wonderful, then you might as well be kind. But kindness is not an insignificant virtue; in fact, it is a potent tool for transformation since it prompts us to step outside our own conditioned response patterns.

I live in Massachusetts, and also sublet a small apartment in New York City for periods when I'll be teaching there. I was at my primary home in Massachusetts in late October of 2012, when hurricane Sandy hit the East Coast. In Massachusetts, we had a power outage of a few hours. As soon as I was plugged in again, I tried to find out what was happening in my New York City neighborhood, Greenwich Village. Of course there was no power at all there, and the outage lasted six full days.

From my now fully lit house in Massachusetts, I considered what that meant. My New York apartment is on the eighth floor. No elevator. No functioning refrigerator. No running water. No heat. I have a neighbor on the eighth floor in a wheelchair. I was quite concerned about him.

Seven days later, when I walked into the building, I asked the doorman about my neighbor. The doorman said, "We all took care of him. We all pitched in and we all took care of one another." He added, "I came in to work every day." I knew, without subways and with gas rationing, this was no easy task. I asked how he'd done that, and he replied, "I borrowed a car, and I got here every day, whatever it took." I saw a second doorman later, and he said, "I had power where I live, but I knew I had to stay here. I felt so bad for the people sitting in the dark, in the cold. I went home once to change clothes, otherwise I just stayed here to help."

I was struck by the simplicity with which they said this. It was simply the right thing to do. It was the *kind* thing to do. So they did it, even though it wasn't easy or convenient or quick. This is the power of compassion. A friend who lives in a building near mine, on the seventeenth floor, with her ninety-two-year-old father, said it was just awful, but it wasn't long before, as she put it, "teams of young people" started coming regularly up the stairs, knocking on doors, asking if people were okay, if they could get them food or water. In many places, people on their own, or in small groups, were moved by compassion to honor a larger sense of humanity and looked out for one another. No matter how many stairs were involved.

DISCONNECTION

There are times when we rise above our normal limitations, but other times we can be so preoccupied with ourselves and defensive against others that kindness is reduced to a veneer of civility. We forget how connected to one another we are, and it is this perceived division that creates alienation. This limited perspective prompts responses that are less creative, and with fewer possibilities for happiness.

Nancy, a copy editor at a daily newspaper, comes up against the limits of her own compassion on a daily basis:

"We publish three editions a day—print and online—and there's a lot of tension in the newsroom as deadlines loom. Missing a deadline brings resentment and recrimination—and the search for someone to blame. I used to get defensive when I was yelled at. Now after meditating for more than five years, I finally see that it doesn't make sense to spend valuable time trying to assign blame. Instead of protecting my self-image of perfection, I try to see what needs to be done and how I can help it get done. I know that other people face consequences if their work is late, so I don't take it personally when they get frustrated. If I understand the problem, I don't add to it. My loving-kindness meditation often involves people at work. I find that helps me see them as people, not jobs, and when I see the humans in the jobs, I respond with more patience and care. Two of the three

Stealth Meditation

At the beginning of a phone call, silently offer the phrases of loving-kindness to all others on the call.

other editors at my level have adopted a similar attitude (one is also a meditator). We offer help, whether it's our direct responsibility or not. We don't panic, don't blame or yell. As a result, the atmosphere has become a lot more calm and pleasant.

"The fourth editor, however, frequently shows up as the difficult person in my loving-kindness meditation. Everything is personal. Everything is suffering. And she sits next to me. After I began meditating, the first thing I noticed regarding her is that I stopped feeding her negativity. I listened to her complaints, but without comment. I stopped getting hooked into her story lines. This took place over a couple of years. Now I offer alternatives. I get less worked up about her attitude, which makes my life happier. I'm more curious and less confrontational. And I understand now how my attitude affects other people."

There's a lot to be learned from Nancy's example. When we stop taking other people's behavior personally, we strengthen loving-kindness. Cultivating an awareness of common ground, we harvest the seeds of compassion. Spending extended periods of time with people whose company we might not voluntarily choose makes us more patient and tolerant. Vulnerability in the face of constant change is something we all share; understanding this, we can respond from the heart. Loving-kindness meditation allows us to use our own pain and the pain of others as a way to connect; looking beyond immediate conflict, we recognize universal suffering and the desire to be happy.

I'm not suggesting that tolerance at work is easy. But loving-kindness often elicits unexpected results when anger threatens to close the heart. Meredith has found a way of avoiding unnecessary conflict at her office by reminding herself that her colleagues are just people like her who want to be happy. "While I try to find something to like about everybody I work with—there are times when it's frustrating," Meredith admits. "If I'm in a conversation with someone and they're not getting it or they're shutting down or bringing up all the things that will go wrong and why it won't work, I can feel myself start to get crazy. Recently, however, a couple of times when this happened I've been at least conscious of that point where they are officially bugging me. I now know that when that happens I have to try to get the conversation finished as quickly as possible. It's a case-by-case situation, but I'm getting better. I don't lock horns the way I used to."

Anger is the opposite of loving-kindness. Anger pushes us to lash out against what's happening in a determination to remain separate from it. Often, anger makes the moment seem even more unbearable ("I can't stand another minute of this!"), showing up in many guises: impatience, anxiety, disappointment, fear, hostility, guilt, aggression. A lot of the time, we are liable to misunderstand anger and our responses to it. Anger can devastate our well-being and strand us far from where we actually want to be. Lost in this state, we can find ourselves without solid ground or a foundation on which to find happiness, stuck with tunnel vision, and unable to find our way back to openheartedness.

Anger is not without its uses, of course. When confronted by unfair or manipulative behavior, anger can help us say no, insist on better treatment, or energize our determination to devise corrections. Anger at our own destructive patterns (also known as exasperation) can jump-start valuable changes in behavior. But skillful use of anger is the exception rather than the rule, as a student of mine, A. Gupta, learned in his compassionate crusade to fight injustice in the legal system:

"I am an attorney by profession, and I work in the very small but growing field of enabling innovation within our criminal justice system. I witnessed firsthand how black and Latino children were being sentenced to months and years of prison for nonsensical offenses such as breaking someone's cell phone and trespassing, or pleading guilty to ramped up charges that would forever remain on their record, hindering simple life opportunities such as getting a mortgage, an education loan, or employment.

"The phenomenon of 'mass incarceration' and the business of the 'prison industrial complex' became crystal clear to me. For years, I was angry. It should not be like this! I was going to fight it! And I took the energy of this anger into other aspects of my life—my interactions with my friends, family members, colleagues, and acquaintances—most of whom are clueless about politics and the legal profession altogether. Simultaneously I witnessed the toll my anger, frustration, and hatred took on me and those I love dearly. I repeatedly created interpersonal dynamics that fostered heartache, verbal violence, hatred, and guilt.

"But this is where my mindfulness practice came to me as a savior. Beneath that anger, what I longed for was a beautiful vision for justice, for peace, for equality, and for fraternity between all beings. But what kept me from reaching that tender space of peace and true compassion for all beings was 'the shoulds' such as 'I should be able to fix this; the system should serve society rather than hobble it.' My daily meditation practice has profoundly transformed my relationship with the work I do, with the values I carry, and the vision I have for the world. Instead of focusing on the bad guys, I aim my anger at the real problems themselves. Mass incarceration is real. Racism is real. Policy decisions based on stereotypes of certain communities are real. Greed is real. Hatred is real. Delusion is real.

"Mindfulness helps me keep my focus on the problems instead of the shoulds. I do my best not to go down the lanes of anger, frustration, and 'it shouldn't be like this' as I did in the past. To this day, the images of young people being recycled in and out of the prison system, and the heartache this causes families and communities nationwide, bring tears to my eyes. But now I am able to place a hand on my heart and say 'sadness is here,' instead of wasting my compassion on rage. I send all those boys, their families, even the prison guards and policy makers, so much love. And I am able to carry on with what I was called in this life to do."

Anger—however natural—narrows the mind and shuts down the heart, more often than not, leaving us confused, antagonistic, and resentful. Mindfulness opens up a world of options for how to work with anger in ourselves, and others, and return to a state of emotional balance. Lenore works within the same prison system that A. Gupta is challenging. She describes her experience this way: "The incarcerated population likes to play games and push as many buttons as possible, and the security staff can be even worse. I make it a point never to make a decision from an emotional place, which is most often one of anger. The difficulty is learning to allow yourself to be humble. In the prison environment, humility is considered a weakness and the trick is to turn it into a strength, to appear stronger to those around me. Every day when I walk the two flights to where the inmates are housed, I do my walking meditation down the steps, to give me focus, calm, and a center before entering into the lion's den. It works surprisingly well."

When we enter high pressure situations with poise and an open heart, we deflect the stress of our surroundings and bring well-being to others, rather than fear or anger. Indeed, the practice of loving-kindness can render us far stronger and more adventurous than we might have imagined. Business Insider program director, Arden Pennell, says "The most valuable thing that I have done in my career to date is have a meditation practice." She describes an intensive loving-kindness meditation retreat she did at the Insight Meditation Society in Barre, Massachusetts. "I had this one moment on

Stealth Meditation

Begin the day with a resolve. "Today I will become more aware of one particular action." Then place your attention on that action throughout the day. Some simple suggestions: opening doors, greeting customers or clients, handwriting, reaching for the phone.

retreat—where you become hyperaware of your mind . . . there's nothing to distract you. So I'm standing in line for lunch thinking, *If I take a double serving of this lasagna, how is that going to look?* And then I had this moment where I thought, *You know, it doesn't really matter what they think of me. I just want them to be happy.*"

Arden goes on to describe, "And it was this profound moment where the mind-state went from insecurity to fear to just wanting the people around me to be well and to be happy. It went from relating to other people as people who could judge me or I had to be anxious around, to just feeling warmer toward them. . . ." Additionally, she describes, while in that mode of loving-kindness, that she decided to email a leader in her field about a posting he'd written that she really admired. "Normally I might have been hesitant to reach out because [he] has a very strong personality and it might be intimidating. But I was in this 'no-fear' state. So I thought, *Oh, this is so cool, I'm going to email him and tell him that I appreciate that he wrote this.* So I did, and that started more of an exchange. And then at some point, he said he was doing a conference and I should really work on it. Helping them launch [that conference] helped me launch my career, but none of this would have happened if I hadn't gone and sat in the woods for ninety-six hours and reached out about an article that I liked. There are a bunch of moments like that in my career that I look back on and see that they trace back to a particular attitude that I can relate to meditation practice."

Because the development of loving-kindness moderates automatic, reflexive fear, it enables us to first, see there might be more doors open for us than we had previously imagined; and second, walk right up to them and often through them.

SELF-BLAME AND COMPASSION

Remorse is a healthy reaction to willfully bad behavior—such as the uncalled-for remark to a colleague or cheating on your time sheet. But no one can be expected *not* to make mistakes. Nevertheless, we heap scorn on ourselves for not being perfect or falling short of our own and others' expectations. Rather than learning from our mistakes and strengthening the intention not to repeat them—viewing our faults and frailties as human qualities worthy of our compassion—we waste time getting caught in spirals of judgment. We seem to believe that if we just condemn and brutalize ourselves enough, with sufficient contempt, we will somehow grow from this punishment.

But is this how we actually learn? Do we learn when we are feeling berated either by ourselves or others? Is this the ideal environment for self-improvement? When we respond to our intrusive thoughts as unwanted visitors whose presence has no reflection on our deepest sense of who we are, we break the cycle of self-contempt. We switch from self-blame to greater acceptance of our crisis of the day. Rather than telling ourselves what losers we are, we soften the internal monologue.

Let's say you forget, again, how to use the new company web-site and are forced to call IT, again, to walk you through it. You can excoriate yourself as a dimwit, worry about your memory loss, or dial your judgment back to a gentle whisper. *Ah, it's you again. Distraction. Fear of technology. Mental fatigue. I wasn't expecting you to embarrass me, again, but now you have, so why not take a hike? Or if you absolutely must stay, how about a cup of tea. Just relax. Take a load off your feet. But stay out of my way.*

One of the greatest skills we can develop is the confi-dence to not relinquish our inner home when we hear the knock of anger at the door of our mind and see that difficult visitor wanting to take over. We can learn to open the door, recognize with awareness what's happening, have compassion and balance, and not confuse the visiting mental state with who we are. In doing this, we are committing to a form of virtue: the goal of not harming ourselves. This is a dynamic practice because it must be continually renewed. We commit to having compassion for ourselves. We're not perfect, we make mistakes, but then we learn to start over.

We need to overcome the false idea that we shouldn't ever be frightened, vulnerable, or depressed, or that we ought to be free of so much pain. The more we spiral down into self-flagellation, the harder it is to focus on the support that is actually there. We lose ourselves in fear of the situation and the judgment of others. Meditation enables us to separate reality from our thoughts *about* reality.

Emily Alp, a writer-editor based in Qatar, in the Persian Gulf, finds this useful when self-blame threatens to overwhelm her. "When things happen at work that used to cause me great anxiety, panic, and tension, I now feel more grounded. I can *choose* how to think with greater ease. Being distanced from my feelings and thoughts in a healthy way, I also make much better choices. I choose to let go a lot more. Rather than obsess about things beyond my control, I say, 'I'll do what I can to make it right for me and for others, but that is all I can do.' I can also say no to projects that others push onto me inappropriately. This gives me more compassion for colleagues who can't do this because they don't know where the line is for themselves."

Psychologist Kristin Neff, author of the book *Self-Compassion,* makes an important distinction between self-esteem and self-compassion. She points out that self-esteem depends on measuring ourselves against whatever standard we deem *the* metric, undefined though it may be—such as am I good enough? smart enough? talented enough? and so on. The difference is that self-compassion is unconditional. When self-compassion is present, our hearts open *more* toward ourselves when we feel down rather than rejecting ourselves as failures. Self-esteem implies feelings of competition and can forsake us in hard times. Self-compassion is self-sustaining, present for us regardless of changing circumstances. It teaches us that when we make mistakes, we have a choice about how we treat ourselves. Rather than loading on judgment and blame, identifying yourself with

Stealth Meditation

Stop and follow your breath for a few moments as you're heating up your lunch in the microwave. The *ding* is your conclusion.

the error with thoughts like: *You're so stupid for sitting through that whole meeting and not uttering a word!*, you can use suffering to inspire a poignant remembrance of human frailty. *I thought keeping quiet would help me get along with my colleagues, but I was wrong. I was coming from a place where I knew so much less about them and about myself than I know now.* Neff describes self-compassion as having three components: mindfulness, a sense of common humanity, and kindness.

MINDFULNESS

This involves bringing awareness to the painful emotions that arise due to our self-judgment or difficult circumstances. We become more accepting and nonjudgmental of our experience, taking a balanced approach so that feelings are neither suppressed nor exaggerated.

COMMON HUMANITY

Our experience is connected to the larger human experience. Being human means being imperfect, and all people have these sorts of painful experiences. Suffering and personal inadequacy are part of the shared human experience—something that we all go through rather than being something that happens to "me" alone.

KINDNESS

This entails being warm and understanding toward ourselves when we suffer, fail, or feel inadequate, rather than ignoring our pain or flagellating ourselves with self-criticism. Being imperfect, failing, and experiencing life's difficulties is inevitable, so we can work to be gentle with ourselves when confronted with painful experiences rather than get angry when life falls short of real or imagined ideals.

Self-compassion is complex, nuanced, and real; an evolving part of a living system—much more like real life, within which we operate with limited information and personal bias, all the while trying to do better.

PRAISE AND BLAME

We cannot be compassionate toward ourselves or others when our personal sense of well-being depends on universal acceptance and praise. When we base our happiness on other people's opinions of us, we're subject to the seesaw of ambivalence, rejection, injustice, and adoration that tips this way or that depending on who likes us and who doesn't in any given moment, or on what someone else is enjoying or enduring.

The first book I wrote was called *Lovingkindness.* From the time I was a child, I had wanted to be a writer, but wasn't confident it would ever actually happen. Finally, the book was done, it was published, and soon after it came out, I was in California. I was having lunch with someone who said, "Sharon, you wrote that book in such a way that it is just like being with you. It is like sitting down and having a conversation with you." I was awash with delight at hearing that. I thought there was no greater compliment one could pay an author. I was so jazzed by the comment that that evening, having dinner with a different group of people, I brought up the comment. Someone at the dinner table said, "Well that's not true. I'm reading the book, and it doesn't sound at all like you. It's nothing like being with you."

I took a breath and reminded myself: You can be ecstatic at lunch and depressed at dinner, or you can take a moment and remember, it's one book! It was written from whatever was motivating me, with whatever level of skill I could bring forth. One person took it one way, another person another way. Not to imply that I didn't notice the difference! Of course we notice, and we care. Who doesn't prefer praise to blame? But the question becomes, how much do we care? The shifting winds of praise and blame will always exist, however carefully or skillfully we act.

Performance reviews are a given for many employees, and can be a picture-perfect supplier of praise and blame. We can use them to better understand our work and our colleagues, or they can become sledgehammers with which we can hit ourselves in yet another way.

Betty says, "I read my annual performance review with a mixture of dread and anticipation. It's like how you'd feel walking on the edge of a cliff. Too close and it's 'good-bye cruel world!' Too far back and you don't get the breathtaking view. In the corporate environment that I have worked in for more than twenty years now, a year's worth of hard work, long hours, and applying yourself diligently to complex problems is distilled into three categories of performance. They are: 1) You are an angel from heaven! We LOVE you and how can we keep you? 2) You didn't screw up and you worked hard. We LIKE you; you can stay. 3) You're a deadbeat. Please leave.

"In two of the twenty years, I had been rated an angel. Both those years had been stellar in terms of environment and opportunities, but most important was the support and trust I had from my leaders and managers who relied on me. The rest of the years I got the second rating and struggled to see why I wasn't rated an angel again, although I had worked so hard and made my bosses so successful.

"This year it was the second rating again. The words in my review were great, such as "strong year, expert, reliable, delivers on time," and yet the rating was that I was not an angel. For about five minutes I felt frustrated, angry, and hurt, and then, when I breathed deep and spoke to a friend at work, my head cleared. Later I had a review with my boss, and I pushed hard to ask for specific feedback about what I need to do to be rated as an angel again. To my surprise, he said '*You* have to tell *me* what I need to do.' I—the subordinate—have to guide and counsel my boss—the superior—in what he needs to do to be successful! I actually found it funny. But I am working on it."

In the world of praise and blame, we are constantly being thrown around by reactions to feedback from the outside world. Love for ourselves cannot reliably be dependent on the esteem of others, however. Of course, we care what others think. We want to be appreciated for our strengths and thanked for our acts of kindness. All of us would rather be loved than hated; this is a natural human response. The problem lies in excessive attachment to how others value us—or not. If we look to praise as the sole confirmation of our personal integrity, we may lose sight of our own self-worth at the first hint of disapproval. It's helpful to do an honest appraisal of where personal convictions are rooted. Do they grow from confidence that we are able to do the right thing though it may not be immensely popular, to step forward, speak our minds, and be ourselves regardless of what others say? Or do we hide our true feelings and withdraw into self-judgment when outside opinions are less than friendly? This question is critical in the workplace, where disagreements are bound to happen and sacrificing what we think to be right for the sake of unvarying approval is a sure road to suffering.

By investigating our relationship to praise and blame, we free ourselves from the habit of absorbing the opinions and prejudices of others. This freedom leaves us flexible and open enough to hear criticism that is useful and true instead of rejecting it automatically. Fielding criticism with an open mind, with an eye toward what we might learn from dissent, reminds us that humility sets us free, that we will never be perfect, and that everyone is in the same fragile boat. The absence of defensiveness leads to less reactivity toward people who judge and blame us. This could not be more important than at work where conflicts abound and professional maneuvering—the do-si-do of getting ahead—can induce a sense of danger, watching your back, over-worrying disapproval, and obsessing over colleagues' admiration. The truth is that there might always be someone who unloads their negativity on us, and sometimes, if we're not mindful, vice versa. What matters is that we approve of ourselves; when we are at peace with our own intention and the quality of the work we're doing. If so, we're less likely to be thrown by rises and dips in our own reputation.

A friend of mine who teaches writing learned this the hard way. An author who spent decades working alone, Michael began giving classes, meeting students, and putting himself into the world in a new, more public way when he was in his fifties. During his honeymoon period as a teacher, he found himself amazed by all the flattery coming at him from adoring students. "It was a whole new kind of egotism," he admits. "Before, when people praised my books or writing, they weren't really praising *me*," explains Michael. "When I started teaching, the adulation felt more personal—and more seductive."

Michael's professional honeymoon came to a crashing end soon enough. "Within a couple of months, I had three students turn against me—viciously," he says. "I didn't realize that there would be a backlash to encouraging my writing students to explore their inner demons," Michael says, chuckling. "The first student blamed me for putting her back on Prozac. The second student got a crush on me and blamed me for leading her on, which is ridiculous since I'm gay. Finally, the third student—the angriest of all—stormed out of our writing group in a rage after I challenged her truthfulness in a memoir, telling me that I'd 'transgressed her boundaries' by asking her to be so honest. She just hated me, that last one, for which I was certainly not prepared."

Blame from this student caused Michael to doubt himself. Though he showed no reaction to her, he was inwardly angry, defensive, and wounded. He realized that if he wanted to continue teaching, he needed to find a middle path between praise and blame—a balanced place of confidence and humility. "Some students love me," Michael understands now. "And others cannot stand me. The difference is, I can live with that now. Teaching is not a popularity contest, though all of us want to be liked. This incident helped me get clear that teaching is not about me at the end of the day. It's about my students and their writing. I'm just a guide and facilitator."

When praise and blame no longer oppress us, we're capable of working with far less stress; we no longer confuse who we are with what we do. We remember that being and doing are different, and that being judged for the job we do has little to do with our true self. Allowing ourselves to "be" at work, we remember that we're more than our reputation or position. We're human beings who want to be fulfilled and free, at work and in the rest of our lives. Loving-kindness can take us there.

Stealth Meditation
Mentally acknowledge those who have helped you learn the skills you have, who have taught you to be better at your job. We are all part of a larger picture.

CORE MEDITATION: Loving-Kindness

The bookends of this practice are to begin a session with offering loving-kindness to ourselves, and end with a more global sense of offering loving-kindness to all. What you do in the middle of those two is really up to you, and might change each day. The meditation below is the core loving-kindness meditation, and what follows that includes suggestions for what you might focus on in that middle section.

Sit, or lie comfortably on your back, eyes closed or open. Offer loving-kindness to yourself by saying silently, "May I be safe. May I be happy. May I be healthy. May I live with ease." Repeat the phrases inwardly at a pace that is pleasing to you, focusing your attention on one phrase at a time. If you find your attention wandering, begin again. Allow your feelings, thoughts, or memories to come and go. Here the anchor is not your breath but the repetition of these traditional phrases. Call to mind someone who has helped you or been good and kind to you. Picture the person, say their name to yourself, get a feeling of their presence, and offer the phrases of loving-kindness to them. Even if the words of the phrases feel strange or awkward, recognize that they're the vehicles for connection. Call to mind someone you know who's having a difficult time right now. Picture them and say their name to yourself, get a feeling of their presence, and offer the phrases of loving-kindness to them: "May you be safe. May you be happy. May you be healthy. May you live with ease."

Or call to mind a neighbor or someone you see fairly often but don't know very well. Picture them, get a feeling of their presence, and wish them well. Call to mind someone you have trouble getting along with. If you pick a difficult person but find that sending them loving-kindness is too hard, then just go back to sending loving-kindness to yourself. In that moment, you're the one who is suffering, so you're worthy of some compassionate attention. Finally you can offer the force of loving-kindness to all beings everywhere, known and unknown, near and far. "May all beings be safe. May all beings be happy. May all beings be healthy. May all beings live with ease." When you feel ready, you can end the session. See if you can bring loving-kindness into your day. Find a few opportunities for silent repetition of these phrases for yourself and for the people around you.

<hr />

MEDITATION: Seeing the Good

Even though our tendency might be to remember the things we've done wrong, the mistakes we've made, and the things we regret, we can consciously shift our attention to include the good within ourselves. We can also do this when we look at others. After a day at work we might recall the late delivery, the disappointing report, the ambiguous commentary. This is not an exercise meant to deny that anything is wrong or regrettable, but if we look at somebody and we think only about the mistakes they have made, then a tremendous sense of self, and other, and us and them, can be reinforced. Whereas if we include even one good thing, if we can think of it, then a bridge is built, so that when we honestly and directly look at what's difficult, it's more from a stance of being side by side rather than across this huge gulf of seeming separation.

Seat yourself in a relaxed, easy posture, however you feel comfortable, and think of one good thing you did yesterday. It may not

A Special Note on Loving-Kindness
for a Difficult Person

When you resolve to send loving-kindness to a difficult person, choose someone mildly troublesome or with whom you're in a bit of conflict. Start with someone relatively manageable because you need to be able to observe your reactions without being overwhelmed. Do the practice as an exploration that allows you to look gently at yourself and see all the ways you might be holding back your compassionate attention or holding on to set ideas about the person in question.

Sometimes anger brings clarity, cutting through niceties, denial, and pretense. But often it leads to delusion and we get caught in a very narrow definition of who we are, and who this other person is, and we forget that change is possible. If you find yourself feeling angry, try to recall the limitations you've previously experienced in this state and how they have kept you from seeing the bigger picture.

We often confuse letting go of anger with letting go of values, but that's not what needs to happen. We can maintain the clarity

~~~~~~

have been very big or grandiose. Maybe you smiled at somebody; maybe you were starting to get annoyed at a slow shop clerk, but you let go of your irritation. Remember that it's not conceited or arrogant to consider what you've done right—it's replenishing to delight in the good that moves through us. Sit with the recollection of what you did right. If you can't think of something good that of our views without getting lost in anger's fixation or feeling a loss of perspective or destructive and damaging actions. Loving-kindness for a difficult person is about seeing what happens when we recognize a connection with someone instead of focusing on the conflict. When we pay attention to that person's suffering, we can look differently at their transgressions.

As you become more comfortable with the practice, you can do it with some ease of heart and even extend loving-kindness to someone who has hurt you more powerfully. The phrases you use might have to be crafted carefully so that you don't feel a tremendous struggle. Try out your own versions of the fol-lowing: "May you be filled with loving-kindness. May you have happiness and the causes of happiness, such as clarity and kind-ness. May you be free of suffering and the causes of suffering, such as ill will and envy. May you be free of anger, enmity, and bitterness."

Sending loving-kindness to a difficult person is a process of relaxing the heart and freeing yourself from fear and corrosive resentment. We are working on our own timeline.

~~~~~~

you did, that's okay. Sitting down to do this meditation is a way of befriending ourselves, and a willingness to expand our awareness, step out of some ruts, and try something new.

Next, think of a benefactor—someone who's helped you. Maybe a mentor at work or an inspiring figure, even if you've never met them. Their good qualities might come in a rush. You can appreciate that about them, those aspects, those efforts, those acts of kindness. Think of a good friend and all that's good within that person, and how much you appreciate that goodness. Think of someone you know who's having a difficult time right now. Focus on the good within them. Maybe the times they've reached out to help others, or their own potential sources of strength. You can see that this person is not just their problem, but something bigger. Think of someone you have a little bit of difficulty with, some conflict, distress. See if you can find some good reflected in things they've done, the choices they've made. And if not, you can switch to another reflection. Remember that, just like each one of us, they want to be happy. Everybody wants the same sense of belonging, feeling at home in this body, this mind, this life. But ignorance is a very strong force. We all have strong habits that lead us far away from happiness sometimes.

Close with staying on the reflection that everybody wants to be happy. "All beings want to be happy; may they be happy." Then silently repeat those phrases. When you're ready, end the meditation. Did you get a glimmer that there might be more room for a fuller perspective on things? That bigger sense of space is equanimity. Having equanimity doesn't mean that we never get overwhelmed or exhausted; it means we work with our attention to remind ourselves of our options when we are having a rough time. When we're having an ordinary day, we remember that we have a resource that allows us to be generous to ourselves and acknowledge our connection to the human community.

EXERCISE: Exploring Self-Compassion

Part One:

Try keeping a daily self-compassion journal for one week (or longer if you like). At some point during the evening when you have a few quiet moments, review the day's events. In your journal, write down anything at work that you felt bad about, anything for which you judged yourself, or any difficult experience that caused you pain. For instance, perhaps you got angry at a colleague because she took forever to reply to your question. You made a rude comment and stormed off. Afterward, you felt ashamed and embarrassed.

How does this aspect of yourself make you feel inside? Scared, sad, depressed, insecure, angry? This is just between you and the paper, so please try to be as emotionally honest as possible and avoid repressing any feelings, while at the same time not being overly melodramatic. Try to just feel your emotions exactly as they are—no more, no less—and then write about them.

Part Two:

Now imagine a fantasy friend who is unconditionally loving, accepting, kind, and compassionate; a friend who can see all your strengths and all your weaknesses, including the aspect of yourself you have just been writing about. He or she loves and accepts you fully. Reflect upon what this friend feels toward you, and how they love and accept you exactly as you are with all your very human imperfections. This friend recognizes the limits of human nature and is kind and forgiving toward you.

Write a journal entry to yourself from the perspective of this imaginary friend, focusing on the perceived inadequacy you tend to judge yourself for. What would this friend say to you about your "flaw" from the perspective of unlimited compassion? How would this friend convey the deep compassion he or she feels for the pain you feel when you judge yourself so harshly? And if you think this friend would suggest possible changes you should make, how would these suggestions embody feelings of unconditional understanding and compassion? For each event, use mindfulness, a sense of common humanity, and kindness to process the event in a self-compassionate way.

After writing the entry, put down your journal for a little while. Then come back and read the entry again, really letting the words sink in. Feel the compassion as it pours into you, soothing and comforting you like a cool breeze on a hot day. Notice that compassion doesn't preclude change and understanding. You can still resolve to behave better.

Practicing the three components of self-compassion—mindfulness, a sense of common humanity, and kindness—with this writing exercise will help organize your thoughts and emotions, while helping to encode them in your memory. If you keep a journal regularly, your self-compassion practice will become even stronger and translate more easily into daily life.

～～～～～

EXERCISE: Moving from Me to We

Bring someone to mind, a fellow human being, just like you. Now silently repeat any number of these phrases, while thinking of them:

- This person has a body and a mind, just like me.
- This person has feelings, emotions, and thoughts, just like me.
- This person has, in his or her life, experienced physical and emotional pain and suffering, just like me.
- This person has at some point been sad, disappointed, angry, or hurt, just like me.
- This person has felt unworthy or inadequate, just like me.
- This person worries and is frightened sometimes, just like me.
- This person has longed for friendship, just like me.
- This person is learning about life, just like me.
- This person wants to be caring and kind to others, just like me.
- This person wants to be content with life, just like me.
- This person wishes to be free from pain and suffering, and to be safe and healthy, just like me.
- This person wishes to be happy and loved, just like me.

Now allow some wishes for well-being to arise:

- I wish for this person to have the strength, resources, and social support to navigate the difficulties in life with ease.
- I wish for this person to be free from pain and suffering.
- I wish for this person to be peaceful and happy and loved.
- Because this person is a fellow human being, just like me.

Q & A

Q My boss is rude and arrogant. He seems to respect me only when I behave that way. I'm afraid that I'll be seen as a wimp if I focus on being more compassionate. How can I mesh the desire to improve with this unpleasant expectation?

A To be able to have compassion means we have some perspective, which is, in fact, our greatest strength. Practicing kindness doesn't mean letting people walk all over us. Responding to rudeness from a motivation of kindness is not the same thing as letting someone's rudeness rule the interaction. It does mean that we are not caught in a downward spiral of resentment and revenge. Experiment with being clear and firm, but not soaking up your boss's attitude. When we don't have to wring out the toxicity of someone else's issues all the time, compassion provides more inner balance so that we can be very strong without the angry reaction.

Q How do I learn to let go of brooding resentment toward a colleague?

A The feeling of resentment isn't the core of the issue—feelings arise without our bidding. I'd like you to consider another aspect. We have so many ideas of what brings us strength, what makes us safe, and what brings us happiness. In particular, the idea that continual resentment or bitterness as a source of power is worth exploring. When you think about it, you might discover that your resentment comes from thinking you've missed an opportunity that should have been yours, but went to another, or that if you're angry enough about this person's perceived transgressions, at least you won't feel weak. In reality, there is not a finite amount of good stuff that is spread among the world—his or her good luck does not mean yours is reduced. And our resentment, as we hang on to it and nurture it, is not going to transform the other person. If we steadily dwell in resentment, we will ensure only that *we* have a really bad day.

Q **There are some people at work I feel I have wronged. I chose one of them to offer loving-kindness to, but it was confusing because I feel that I was the difficult person in the dynamic. What should I do?**

A In formal meditation practice, we look at which is more helpful for changed behavior: endlessly castigating ourselves for a mistake or learning how to begin again. We can apply that knowledge to our work life as well. Regret can be a good, helpful spur toward change, but not being able to ever move beyond it can be exhausting and debilitating.

It's useful to look at the situation with a big perspective. Is there anything you can do to make amends? Would it be useful to apologize? Are there other ways you can help someone out? And in meditation, try switching between offering loving-kindness to yourself and to this other person, back and forth, because you have both been affected by your behavior.

Q When difficult things happen, how can I balance compassionate openheartedness with discernment—or seeing a situation for what it truly is—so that my actions don't feel like acquiescence?

A There are lots of different kinds of balances we look for in the workplace. We look for a balance between compassion for ourselves and compassion for others. We look for a balance between compassion and equanimity, between a caring heart and realizing we can't just fix everything for someone. We need both compassion and discernment, or wisdom, in full measure for any of these to develop. Compassion should never mean giving up discernment, and vice versa.

CHAPTER 4

Resilience

N O JOB IS STRESS FREE. No working life comes without challenges, conflicts, pressures, setbacks, or moments of sheer exhaustion. Happiness at work depends on our ability to cope with the obstacles that come our way and to bounce back, learn from mistakes, make amends when necessary, and—most important of all—*begin again* without rumination or regret. This is perhaps the greatest lesson of meditation and all mindfulness practice. That no matter what the circumstances, we are always able to begin again in a new moment. This is what we mean by resilience. No matter what happens to us at work (or elsewhere), we can learn to use challenges as opportunities to grow, increase our awareness, and learn methods for making future challenges more tolerable.

PRACTICING SELF-CARE
TO AVOID BURNOUT

As many as half of all workers in high-stress occupations suffer from some form of burnout during their career. Although stress, anxiety, and depression may coexist, burnout is a distinct condition of exhaustion characterized by a loss of motivation, fatigue, frustration, anger, depression, and dissatisfaction that if untended can grow to severe proportions.

A growing body of research shows that strategic renewal, including midday rest, longer sleep hours, more time away from the office, and more frequent vacations will boost productivity, job performance, and health. A recent study of four hundred employees found that sleeping too little—less than six hours a night—was one of the best predictors of on-the-job burnout. The human body is not designed to expend energy continuously. Our bodies regularly tell us to take a break, but we often override these signals and counter fatigue with stimulants including coffee, sugar, and so on.

If we don't work in an environment that supports more vacation time, midday breaks, and more time away from the office, we can use tools like the ones offered in this book to accomplish that relief and renewal within ourselves. In many places, we will have to.

Ellen's job is an example of this kind of place. "I work at a school for students who are diagnosed with everything from mild anxiety to full-blown schizophrenia. I am often in a classroom full of emotional expressions including anger, anxiety, muteness, screaming, throwing chairs, tuning out with an iPod, tears and more tears. It is a chaotic environment and structure is needed. After one week of working here, a teacher knows that consistency is the key. The students need rules and must rely on the adults to enforce them. We start every new year full of determination that this year will be better than the last, that *we* will be better than last year. But we get pummeled every time.

"There is a blue binder that we receive in the beginning of every year and we have to return it at the end of the school year. It is the policies and procedures handbook—the rule book! At first, it felt good to have a rule book, so that you know what the rules are, what we can and cannot do, what students can expect if they choose a certain behavior—what will be the consequences to their actions. This felt good to have, until you realize that nobody upholds it."

This is the kind of situation where you need inner resources that will enable you to not only survive, but also to find meaning and hope. I asked Ellen how she had done that. She replied, "The only real hope I could see is when those kids sincerely felt that you cared about them and believed they could be better and saw some potential in them. They couldn't do this for themselves. Often, when they went home, their homes were also dysfunctional and their parents also saw them as problems, so they couldn't escape that perception of themselves.

Stealth Meditation
Notice how you are holding something in your hand—a steering wheel or a cup, for instance. What is the quality of your grip? Sometimes we exert so much force holding things, it exacerbates tension without our realizing it.

"But some teachers cared, and that gave them hope. The kids came to school—that was the first step. Some students refused to attend their public school, so coming in at all was a successful day. And they came to school looking for hope, looking for those teachers to tell them again that, 'you are a good writer,' 'you are an amazing artist,' 'with proper care, you can manage your mental health,' 'you are so smart.'

"And we also told them, 'I feel that way, too, sometimes;' 'it is really hard for me to get to work some days, too; I'd rather stay in bed;' 'I used to feel that way, too, when I was a teenager; I was really depressed and couldn't share my feelings.' Telling them the truth, showing them that we can share the same feelings, that our lives are difficult sometimes, too—this gave them a feeling that if I can get up and get here tomorrow morning, so can they.

"I told them that I used to believe that I didn't want to live past twenty years old, that I felt so hopeless about life. But I kept pressing on and by showing up to life and seeking and finding answers that worked for me along the way, I have felt so much happiness, and I am so glad that I didn't give up on life. Knowing these things about me has made a difference to them and, I think, given them hope. And it gave me hope to give them hope!"

This is why I've always believed that it is important for teachers like Ellen to have support, including tools to foster inner resilience and avoid burnout. It is such a hard job, often frustrating and exhausting, but Ellen's openness to the students is what allowed the relationships to be genuine and move them mutually forward. Ellen worked to inspire those students and keep them going, and they did the same for her.

In practice and in action, loving-kindness works best when we include ourselves. One domestic violence shelter worker told me that she was so determined to take a lunch break that she locked the door to her office anticipating some private time. That didn't work, though, because after knocking on the door and getting no answer, her colleagues would peer through the keyhole to see if she was in there. Rather than sacrifice her much needed alone time, she started turning out the light so that no one could see her and she began doing her meditation practice in this dark office with the door locked, and that's how she got some space. Whatever it takes to give yourself some peace and quiet, by all means do it.

THE ILLUSION OF CONTROL

Another reason that we burn out is the false belief that we ought to have greater control over colleagues, bosses, clients, and outcomes than we do. It is only when we question this assumption of control that we begin to see how delusional it really is. Before we heap blame upon ourselves at work, we might learn to ask, "Could I have controlled that? How could I have stopped that from coming up?" More often than not, the answer is that we could not have prevented the unexpected for which we are nonetheless blaming ourselves.

Every job involves setbacks, disappointments, and failures. How we respond to these setbacks is our decision. As Henry Ford put it, "Failure is only the opportunity to begin again more intelligently." Inspired by the 28-day Meditation Challenge from my book *Real Happiness,* a student of mine used her practice to improve a failing scenario at work. As part of a team that was proposing a major marketing campaign for the company, she prepared a complicated report for a new boss who requested several revisions, which infuriated her. When she decided to follow her breath, and let go of the anger, she was able to put aside her pride and anxiety about what the new boss might think of her and see that the boss's comments had been helpful and could improve the project in interesting ways. In the end, the boss was impressed not only by the finished product but by her positive attitude.

"Often if you look a little more deeply into a situation that is upsetting you, you realize you're afraid," Mirabai Bush says. "Learning how to let go of the illusion of control is so important. Notice that your ego is operating and causing these fears and then practice letting go in that moment. This increases a kind of radical self-confidence and introduces you to what's going on inside yourself and in your environment, to help you see things more clearly."

Acceptance—and beginning again—is the essence of all meditation practice. Each time we sit down to meditate, we are starting over. Every time we forget to breathe or our minds wander or we're hijacked by feelings or sensations, we gently bring ourselves back to the breath, again and again. Each opportunity to interrupt the onslaught of thoughts and return to the object of meditation is, in fact, a moment of enlightenment; this principle of starting over—and approaching each challenge or frustration with a beginner's mind—is the essence of resilience. When we don't allow setbacks to defeat us, they become opportunities for learning, acceptance, flexibility, and patience. When we engage a wait-and-see attitude toward outcomes and possibilities, this openness to possibility helps us weather the inevitable adversities of working life.

A key to exploring the myth of control is seeing the many strands of conditioning, influences, and causes that make up any given moment. As parts of a greater whole, we do not orchestrate all the grand motions of the universe. On a good day, we have a measure of control over ourselves—what we choose and how we behave—but beyond that our powers are sadly limited. The awareness of a bigger picture of causes and conditions can ease our habitual, scorching self-blame for inevitable mistakes and disappointments.

I was in New York City once, trying to hail a cab to take me uptown to a lecture by Vietnamese Zen master Thich Nhat Hanh. It was right at the time shifts were changing, when it is typically quite hard to find an available taxi. Some do stop, however, ask where you are going, and if your destination matches the general area they need to go to to turn in the cab and sign out for the day, they'll take you. That's just what happened to me. A driver agreed to take me uptown, and we were on our way. But before too long, we got stuck in unthinkably bad traffic. I don't recall ever seeing such traffic. As we crawled along, trying to go across town, then trying to go uptown, then across town again, trying anything, we barely made any progress. I wondered if I would make it to the talk at all. I felt bad for the cabdriver, wondering if he might get penalized for returning the cab late. I began an apology, "I am so sorry. You were nice enough to pick me up, and now you will be late. I can't believe this monstrous traffic. I've never seen anything like this. I'm so, so sorry." He interrupted me, "Madam, traffic is not your fault." Then he paused a moment, and said, "Nor is it mine."

I just loved that he added, "Nor is it mine." I thought of how many times customers probably blamed him for their own tardiness, for bridge closings and tired toll collectors and wild drivers of other cars. It was such a wonderful teaching that I realized it would be okay if I didn't make it to the lecture at all. (I did, by a second.)

In tough economic times, self-blame and the urge to control outcomes only increase. As competition levels rise and salaries fall, it is easy to feel insufficient, underachieving, and insecure about our professional selves. With so many people losing their jobs, feeling humiliated becomes an increasing hazard. We tend to think of things like unemployment and professional setbacks as disgraceful and personally caused, rather than as part of a whole matrix of conditions that are happening worldwide.

Meditation helps us interrupt the self-flagellating, story-spinning mind that creates these add-ons and the illusion of control. Every career path can, on occasion, take an unexpected turn. Our job can neither rescue us from life's uncertainties nor secure our reputation, identity, or self-worth. By being realistic about what work can and cannot provide us, we can begin to relate with our job properly and precisely and not as a matter of ego survival. Insisting that work provide inner security means that we sometimes find ourselves spending more time and effort holding on to our jobs than actually performing them. Being able to distinguish what work can give us and what we can give to our work reminds us that we are bigger than our jobs. Seeing the many ways we have a choice, in how we respond, how we define ourselves—even when unemployed—makes us resilient.

Melanie, an artist whose financial life perpetually hangs by a thread, has learned to be a master of letting go, moving from one freelance job to the next with a delightful élan and lack of anxiety. She does not see her insecure work status as a disgrace; instead, it is the price she pays for her freedom. "It's ironic," Melanie says. "When I had a full-time job, back in the Stone Age, I lived in fear of losing it. I was so anxious that I must have been the worst midlevel administrator that savings bank had ever seen," she admits with a laugh. "You know how fear compounds itself the more you think about it? Finally, I was so miserably scared, and positive that banking wasn't for me, that I gave my two weeks' notice. I walked away from a paycheck into nothing. But nothing turned out to be just what I needed. Now I work jobs as long as they're working for me—through a temp service—and move on when I feel like it. I take more pride in my work, too, because I'm not so scared of losing it."

Not everyone can up and quit their jobs like Melanie did—nor do all of us pine for a freelance life—but it's always a good idea to stop looking over our shoulder and remember that we can choose how to respond to our circumstances.

PATIENCE AND PERSPECTIVE

That choice of response, once again, fosters resilience. Remaining open to possibilities can give us the flexibility necessary to being happy at work. A flexible approach to resilience is especially vital when dealing with difficult work situations. When we're adaptable, we learn to focus our energy on areas of the job that we can manage and let go of the rest. When we take time to focus on the part of the environment we can control—most particularly ourselves—our working life becomes less emotionally precarious.

Patience is a much underrated tool for dealing with frustrating work situations. The more time we spend on practicing patience, the more rewarding it becomes as the mind is trained to settle down. Patience defines our survival advantage over other animals that are conditioned to react to immediate rewards and are unable to forestall impulsivity. It is our primary means of escaping what sociologist Charles Tilly called "the tyranny of the here and now." Patience at work begins with the full acknowledgment of conditions exactly as they are. This includes the restless, critical, or stubborn states of our own mind. A student of mine was amazed, on the morning of a job interview, when mindfulness practice enabled her to catch herself in the middle of a long-held assumption regarding her confidence and self-worth (*I'm not good enough! I can't compete. I'll never get it!*). Barraged by fear, in the past her mind would have spun out of control and kept her on tenterhooks, and she would have beaten herself up in the interim. Had she not been patient enough to stop, sit quietly, and observe but not become immersed in her self-defeating thoughts, she would never have been able to notice this pattern—and compose herself enough to land the job.

Cultivating a flexible perspective, and the ability to let go, is essential to whatever kind of work we do. As we learn to delay the story lines and mental habits that we typically bring to our work, and simply become available to our circumstances in the moment, we're able to adapt to things as they actually are. Rather than rejecting difficulties as bothersome interruptions, we can instead acknowledge work with all its complications as an invitation to wake up and live our lives more honestly and fully.

If we view the capacity of our minds more expansively, our absorption of change or difficulty can open up as well. No matter what comes our way, mindfulness strengthens our ability to "take it light," attaching ourselves less to outcomes and control, learning to delay immediate gratification, and changing lifelong patterns. This is where neuroscience is helping us to understand how resilience works. The discovery of neuroplasticity—the biological process whereby the brain can be reshaped through practice—shows us that changing habits, such as impatience, actually alter emotion and cognition. It is now believed that many different mechanisms of neuroplasticity persist for our entire life span. This is in stark contrast to when I was younger and in school. Then we were taught that the brain was different from other organs and that we were all born with a fixed complement of cells. The process of development and aging was nothing other than irrevocable cell loss. It was a one-way street. Now it's said that an average adult generates somewhere between five and ten thousand new cells every day. And that happens throughout life until our very last day. So, every day until our last, what we are doing with our mind matters.

> **Stealth Meditation**
>
> Nourish yourself! Eat a meal mindfully, noticing the colors, the flavors, the texture of what you are eating.

Resilience relies on openness. I saw this clearly a few years back when my goddaughter asked me a question about how the mind works. "It's kind of like this," I wrote. "You can have your mind be really, really, big—like the sky. Then, when different things happen—maybe somebody at school says something that hurts your feelings or something really difficult happens for you—it's not that you don't feel it, but your mind is as big as the sky—and it contains your awareness of all the stuff in your life. When you think that way, then the mean things that people say can seem like clouds moving through the sky, and they don't bother you as much. Some people feel as if they have a mind like a sponge. To have a mind like a sponge is to feel like everything everyone says is going to fill you up and you're going to end up all soggy, filled with water, and it's going to be really difficult to do what you want and feel what you want, because you've soaked up everyone else's thoughts and feelings. It can take time and practice to have your mind feel more like the sky than a sponge, but I think it's worth it."

As true as this is for a nine-year-old, it's true for all of us. We can be like the sky or we can be like a sponge. It is out of the greatest generosity toward ourselves that we choose not to live as sponges. It's not out of trying to be a perfect person or some punitive judgment toward who we actually are; it is a great kindness to ourselves when we remember that we have the option of not absorbing every frustration or crisis or hurt. We may not be able to control our changing circumstances or always react the way we want to, but neither must we overreact to them.

When employers establish compassionate policies, understanding that success arises from self-confidence and self-care, a culture of consciousness is created in the workplace. A few years back, Casey Sheahan faced a major challenge. "When the financial crisis began in late 2008, I thought Patagonia might have to conduct layoffs to offset a potential slowdown in business," he remembers. "When I told my wife that I was contemplating a layoff, she asked me, 'Are you making this decision out of fear or love?' I said, 'Fear, of course. Our orders could go down, the market for outdoor apparel could collapse as people focus on their basic needs.' She said, 'And what if you made a decision based on love?' I answered, 'Then I would find other creative ways to lower expenses.' So we did and Patagonia has had four of its best financial years in its history.

"Instead of contemplating layoffs, we found other ways to cut costs. We cut back on product lines that weren't working, unnecessary expenses, and an array of projects that we were involved in that might not be necessary. It was a reflection moment for us as a company. I told my employees, 'Look, we're not going to lose anybody, so we are all going to have to share collectively and be prudent. You're going to spend the company's money as if it were your own and only spend on things that are absolutely necessary to keep the company moving forward.'"

This same principle of creative thinking holds true for workers of all levels. "I had a pretty high-stress job at a company during the middle of the crash of the late nineties when many companies were going public," reports a student of mine named Angela. "There was bad debt, people were getting laid off. It was a tense time." After going through a winter like this, Angela was burned out and "just wanted to be outside." She requested to be laid off instead of quitting (for salary reasons) and found a job as a park ranger for the summer out on Boston Harbor Islands where she had gone camping. Being on Bumpkin Island with no electricity or running water, watching the sunsets every night, was a restorative experience for Angela.

But as the summer came to a close, she didn't know what to do next. She decided to call up her former boss to let him know what was going on, and he asked her to come into work a couple of days a week. Although the thought of returning to the company was not appealing, Angela decided to keep an open mind. In fact, the company itself had undergone some positive changes in her absence and improved its own resilience. "It was a different company," she found. "The atmosphere had become entrepreneurial and far less stressful." Angela found herself enjoying the place and was back working full time within the year. As the company evolved, so did Angela's duties, and her ability to learn new skills, remain open to challenge, and go with the flow, helped her succeed at work. In the fifteen years from then until now, Angela has had at least ten job titles with this company. "Whatever was asked of me, I said yes and then figured it out later," she says. Angela recalls an excellent piece of advice that she received from her father after graduating from college with no idea what to do to earn a living. "He told me, 'There are people who might pay you just to be yourself.'" In this case, being herself meant showing the diversity of her abilities. Angela's willingness to try anything resulted in her not being stuck with one definition of her job. She believes that she's survived— indeed *thrived*—at her company for all these years precisely because of resiliency and patience. "Whatever they wanted to throw my way, I was willing to give it a try!"

RESILIENCE IN THE FACE
OF GREAT PAIN

Several years ago, I went to Walter Reed Army Hospital in Washington, DC, to lead a program for the nurses, as well as to have a tour of one of the wards. It was intense and difficult to witness. The patients seemed so young. I saw so many parents, with faces drawn, trying to encourage their sons to enjoy something—anything. A young wife chastised her husband for having gone to war, as he lay in his hospital bed, his eyes blank. A young man with intractable pain didn't seem to know where to turn. Boys without legs were resolutely walking up and down the corridors on artificial limbs and crutches. Between the patients and their families, it was an emotionally painful place to be. A friend of mine who works there came on the tour of the ward with me and said afterward, "You know, the nurses who can work here are not the ones who get lost in sorrow. The nurses who can stay here are the ones who can connect with the resiliency of the human spirit."

Caregivers of all kinds are especially prone to burnout. A sense of being overwhelmed and unable to continue helping is a condition commonly known as *compassion fatigue.* A strong identification with suffering is often part of the motive for workers in this field. While compassion fatigue is the more common term, Matthieu Ricard, the Buddhist monk and scholar, prefers *empathy fatigue.* Psychologists tell us that while closely related, empathy and compassion can be distinguished.

Empathy, the resonance with what another person is feeling, can be a wonderful building block for compassion. Empathy evokes a sense of sympathy, and compassion evokes a sense of warmth and caring. But when our own dismay at what we are witnessing takes center stage, it can also become what's known as *empathic distress*. Empathic distress evokes a sense of being overwhelmed, exhausted, and depleted.

To show the difference among empathy, compassion, and empathic distress, Dr. Tania Singer has studied Buddhist monks skilled in compassion practice. When the monks watched videos of people suffering, fMRI scans of their brains showed heightened activity in the areas associated with care, nurturing, and positive social attachment. In nonmeditators, however, the videos were more likely to trigger areas in the brain associated with feelings of sadness and pain.

The distinction between empathic distress and compassion is linked directly to decreased happiness levels among physicians and other caregivers. A full *60 percent* of practicing physicians report burnout symptoms, including emotional exhaustion, depersonalization (treating patients as objects), and a low sense of accomplishment. Naturally, this affects how our doctors care for us; the quality of treatment becomes substandard, patient dissatisfaction increases along with medical errors and lawsuits. All of these dynamics, paired with a

Stealth Meditation

Take a few minutes to investigate how you would like to be perceived at the conclusion of a meeting, an email, a call. Would you like to come across as fearsome, gentle, resolute, inclusive, open-minded, unwavering? How do you feel when you perceive others that way?

markedly decreased ability to express compassion, are warning signs of physician burnout.

Empathy fatigue is often compounded exponentially by the shame associated with showing grief and other uncomfortable emotions in a context where it is considered unprofessional. Those caregivers who struggle to manage their grief with the detachment they believe is necessary to doing their job report feelings of failure, self-doubt, sadness, powerlessness, guilt, loss of sleep, and crying. The impact of this unacknowledged pain is exactly what we don't want our doctors, nurses, and other caregivers to experience: inattentiveness, impatience, irritability, emotional exhaustion, and, certainly, burnout.

There is a different kind of detachment that begins with first acknowledging the pain we are witnessing and what we ourselves feel, and learning a different relationship to it. Tucker, a psychotherapist, writes, "I work with people who have suffered severe abuse. When I saw that real life contains things that are so horrifying, my natural reaction had been to "go to sleep," that is, to close down my mind enough that I wouldn't feel the pain. But now I'm trying to open my heart to whatever is happening. There's still this strong drive to "go to sleep," but I've tried that so many times, and I know what happens. If I'm not willing to accept reality with an open heart, no matter what reality looks like, then I can't be present enough to help people whose suffering is so deep. Reality is all we have, so I'm trying to stay open to all of it. Being awake certainly has made me cry more often, but it's an awful lot better than tuning out or turning off when the world isn't the way I think it should be."

If we don't include that step of acknowledgment, our detachment may not be serving us (or those we are trying to help) as a genuine coping skill. It becomes just another way of hiding from how hard things are and how affected we are by all that's going on.

A humanitarian worker named Marianne Elliott learned this in Afghanistan, while observing the avoidance tactics of her coworkers and dealing with her own emotions and ways of coping.

"In the world of humanitarian and development workers in which I live, there is a strong value placed on emotional detachment, the ability to remain coolheaded under any circumstance." Did it ever get to her—all the terrible suffering and feeling as if there is little she can do to prevent it?

"Of course, it's hard. I've been told again and again to stay a bit detached from it, to maintain professional distance, to keep a sense of perspective. Otherwise you can't do your job. I understand what everyone is saying to me, but the pressure to appear emotionally detached feels like denying the part of me that drew me to this work in the first place, the same part that makes me effective in my job. It also seems that 'staying a bit detached' isn't really working for all my colleagues, either. Some of them show signs of chronic anxiety, like facial tics or insomnia. Others get blindingly drunk once a week to 'clear out all the crap,' as one of them put it. One of my housemates retreats into his bedroom as soon as we get home from work and doesn't emerge until the following morning. Apparently, he's playing computer games. All of this may be more socially acceptable in our community than my outbursts of crying, but I am not sure it's what 'coping well' looks like."

In order to meet suffering in an open, yet truly sustainable way for the long haul, we need to stop trying to control it. Otherwise, we are sure to succumb to empathy fatigue. Whether you care for a classroom of young children with special needs, an aging patient, a difficult-to-understand teenager, or a community with no clear resolution to their problems in sight, any skillful caregiving relationship relies on balance: the balance between opening one's heart as much as possible and accepting the limits of what one can do; the balance between compassion and equanimity.

One beautiful definition of compassion that I especially love is "the trembling of the heart in response to suffering." But compassion has its near enemy, which is being swamped by the pain we see. Falling into the near enemy means being exhausted, depleted, feeling we cannot care anymore or even be present in the face of that suffering. Without some measure of balance, we will descend very readily into a state of being overwhelmed.

Equanimity is the spacious stillness that can acknowledge things are the way they are. Equanimity is the voice of wisdom, the articulation of intelligence. It reminds us of what we cannot know right now, what we are not in control of, and what, ultimately, is not in our hands. The perspective granted by equanimity is not indifference. It doesn't mean apathy, it doesn't mean not caring. Equanimity certainly doesn't mean pretending not to care with an assumed, obligatory detachment. Instead, equanimity is a kind of balance that comes from seeing things as they are.

So for example, with great loving-kindness and compassion, we may want someone to heal, to be better, to stop behaving in a self-destructive way, or just to be different. We may want institutions to be less entrenched, communities to be a lot more flexible, and the wheels of justice to spin a lot faster. All of that is natural. Resolve, determination, and commitment are building blocks of our efforts toward change. At the same time, the wisdom that underlies equanimity, tells us, "Yes, I will be there and I will try and I will work, but in the end it's not completely up to me and my will."

This is not our world to singularly create, and it's not our prerogative to insist that a person's suffering just disappear (would that it were!). We need to practice a kind of letting go. Letting go doesn't mean shoving somebody away and denying their distress. It's more like having a really immense picture of life, and a true one, to mitigate our impatience and despair.

True equanimity doesn't weaken our compassion: It actually strengthens it. With equanimity we can be present without being caught in such a ferocious agenda built of our own expectation, our own attachment, our own need for satisfaction. Equanimity endows loving-kindness with patience and endows compassion with courage. It's not easy to be very present with suffering and not fall into despair—to overcome the feeling of our own powerlessness or helplessness at fixing things. Yet we can find this balance, and with it, resilience.

The combination of compassion and equanimity allows us to profoundly care, and yet not become overwhelmed or unable to cope because of that caring. Her time in Afghanistan helped Marianne get to this place of compassion and equanimity. "My Afghan colleagues have taught me there is no shame in tears when they are shed for good reason. Sitting with a woman whose child has been kidnapped by a warlord is a good reason.

Stealth Meditation

Read an entire email twice before composing a response.

Meeting a father who has no food for his children is a good reason. Whenever my colleagues see me in those situations, tears glistening in my eyes as I frantically scribble down all the information I need, they smile approvingly. 'Marianne is compassionate,' they tell each other, 'she feels the pain of our people.' It is true. I do feel the pain of the people I meet in Afghanistan. And in that meeting of sorrow, I have learned that I don't need to fix their problems. That simple lesson, perhaps more than anything else, has finally allowed me to be fully present to the person in front of me. When my mind isn't racing ahead to think of what I can do to help, I'm able to give my full attention to the person who is talking to me. I'm also able to read the subtle messages of the silent participants, the wives, mothers, aunts, daughters, and sisters of the men who are talking."

Loving-kindness for ourselves and others creates the essential caring atmosphere within which resilience can flourish. It's not realistic to think that we can completely overlook ourselves and continue to have the resourcefulness or inner abundance to be able to give to others. And in addition, we tend to isolate when we are overwhelmed rather than connect, when connection is what we need most. In fact, a sense of isolation was one of the burdens many people working in domestic violence shelters described. One of those workers summed it up this way: "I could never go home and tell my partner the stories I hear—not because of confidentiality, but because they are unbearable. How could I put that on him?"

High-risk jobs involving violence or great suffering demand a special kind of compartmentalization. As one police officer puts it, "Your spouse may not really want to hear about the week-old body you had to fish out of the lake." We might need to build a stronger sense of community at work so that we can speak openly about the details of our experience. At the same time, we need to take steps to remain emotionally available to friends and family, so that our witnessing great suffering doesn't leave us feeling cut off and alone. Sometimes reticence is a show of love. Allowing work to stay at work can paradoxically preserve our personal relationships and strengthen our sense of team solidarity on the job. Connection to our own inner strengths, to a community, and to a bigger picture of life engenders resilience.

After struggling with burnout for years, an aid worker named Elie Calhoun eventually discovered a self-care equation that works for him. "I remember three things," says Elie, who has spent long periods of time in refugee camps around the world. "Number one, the work I do is *service*. Number two, service work requires *emotional labor*. Finally, emotional labor requires *rest*. When I see service work for the emotional labor that it is, I understand why I get so exhausted. The more people I connect with, the greater my need for serious downtime." Once again, by realizing that we have a choice in how we treat ourselves and how we wish to be treated, we can better exercise that power and increase our resilience.

A woman who works on the police force expressed this to me beautifully. "In police work, the use of the word 'enemy' can get you into trouble. But the reality for most of us in this line of work is that the real enemy is often unseen and unheard. The enemy isn't really a person. It's the unknown. It's that instant in which the world comes to a halt, when the sight of a dead newborn in the arms of her mother or the mutilated body of a murder victim causes you to struggle to assign normalcy to something so horrible. When knocking on the door of a quaint Craftsman bungalow with news of a loved one's death turns your heart into a heap of insurmountable sadness.

"For many officers, religion plays an important role. Others reason that a loving God couldn't possibly condemn so many with such cataclysmic grief. There are a few of us who balance our spiritual lives, trying to find a 'middle way.' We hope, we practice, we pray, we negotiate. In the end, the enemy will never destroy that indomitable spirit that lies within the heart. It just takes a little patience to get it right."

MEDITATION: Loving-Kindness for Caregivers

Whether you care for a young child in school, aging patients, at-risk teenagers, an anxious client at work whose needs are pressing upon you, or a community that demands a lot of you, any skillful relationship of caregiving relies on balance—the balance between opening one's heart again and again, and accepting the limits of what one can do. The balance between compassion and equanimity. As mentioned earlier, compassion can be thought of as the trembling of the heart in response to suffering. Equanimity is a spacious stillness that can accept things as they are. The balance of compassion and equanimity allows us to care, and yet not get overwhelmed and unable to cope because of that caring.

The phrases we use reflect this balance. Choose one or two phrases that are personally meaningful to you. There are some options offered below. You can alter them in any way, or use others that you have created out of their unique personal significance.

To begin the practice, take as comfortable a position as possible, sitting or lying down. Take a few deep, soft breaths to let your body settle. Bring your attention to your breath, and begin to silently say your chosen phrases over and over again, in rhythm with the breath. You can also experiment with just having your attention settle in the phrases, without using the anchor of the breath. Feel the meaning of what you are saying, yet without trying to force anything. Let the practice carry you along.

- "May I offer my care and presence without conditions, knowing they may be met by gratitude, anger, or indifference."

- "May I find the inner resources to be able to truly give."

- "May I remain in peace and let go of expectations."

- "May I offer love, knowing I can't control the course of life, suffering, or death."

- "I care about your pain, yet cannot control it."

- "I wish you happiness and peace but cannot make your choices for you."

- "May I recognize my limits compassionately, just as I recognize the limitations of others."

Experiment with bringing these phrases into your work with you, and experience the support and balance they help provide.

———————

EXERCISE: Patience

Bring to mind or write down a situation where you felt impatient toward someone. Were you responding only to the incident at hand or can you trace contributing factors that might have helped lead to the impatience? Were you late to work? Unable to find a parking space or a seat on the train? Were you suddenly finding yourself in the grip of the same set of conditions as at your last job? What other factors might have influenced how you felt, thought, behaved?

Were there consequences for you or the other person based on your impatience? How do you feel about what happened? Without the influence of those other factors, how do you think you might have responded?

Now imagine yourself entering that same situation with a calm and open heart, less encumbered by the past, and able to recognize and let go of those other contributing factors. How are you behaving differently? The gap between those two scenarios is the difference between being bound by reactivity and having the freedom to respond rather than merely react.

EXERCISE: Everything That Comes to Mind When It Comes to Stress

On a piece of paper or on your computer, list everything that comes to mind that contributes to stress for you at work. Perhaps budget cuts, a new phone system, too many clients, unclear expectations from your boss. Don't worry if the list becomes quite long.

In another column, list everything you do to restore equilibrium, lift your spirits, get a break. This list might include listening to music, running, spiritual community, reading trashy novels—anything that makes you feel better, happier. Be honest and don't censure yourself, even if you know it's something that might be judged by others. Add a third list which describes how much of an effect each strategy seems to be having on your stressors. Take a look at the lists and reflect on how much you need to cope with, if you are coping well now, or if you need to change some of the ways in which you cope.

EXERCISE: Self-Care

Take a look at each item on the second list you compiled for the previous exercise, the things you do for coping with stress. Evaluate each in terms of how they make you feel, if you want to continue or even strengthen them, or see if perhaps, given an honest look, they actually bring you down and you'd like to replace them. If the latter pertains, what might you replace them with? Notice that with awareness, you become empowered. Are all the activities you do for relief things you do alone? If so, and if that feels like a problem, are there supportive groups you could join?

Q&A

Q   **After I've been taking care of others for some time, I feel a need to replenish and be generous to myself. Is that wrong?**

A   If we're looking to assess the integrity of our actions, looking at our intention is very important. What looks like generosity on the surface may not be coming from a very generous place within. If we're nearing burnout, we may be giving to others out of a sense of obligation, martyrdom, a feeling we ourselves don't deserve anything, or simply habit. And if that is what your mindfulness reveals to you, you very well might need to replenish. This doesn't necessarily mean leaving your job, but rather finding some time and compassion for yourself so that when you are giving to others, it can be genuine, authentic, and with the right intention.

Q   **Please describe a meditation that you can do either to unwind when you get home or to help you fall asleep if it's hard for you to let go of work.**

A   Try this: Sit comfortably or lie down. Bring your atten-
     tion to the top of your head and simply feel whatever
sensations are there—perhaps tingling, vibration, or pulsing.
Perhaps you notice an absence of sensation. Very slowly, let
your attention move down the front of your face, and then
the back of your head. Be aware of whatever you encounter—tightness, relaxation, pressure. Acknowledge whatever
you feel—it may be pleasant, painful, or neutral—in your
forehead, nose, mouth, cheeks, the back of your head. You
needn't name these sensations, just feel them. You don't have
to do anything about them; you're just noticing them.

Then move your attention slowly all the way through
your neck, throat, shoulders, arms and hands, your torso,
until you come to your legs and finally the soles of your feet.

Q   **When I was thinking of a difficult person in my office
     and offering them loving-kindness, I began thinking,
"Wouldn't it be good for the whole team of us if this person
was better?" And that seemed selfish.**

A   That thought is not a sign of selfishness; it's wisdom.
     It is generally out of our own pain or subtle dissatisfac-
tion that we lack empathy and consideration toward others.
The more any one of us can tap into a sense of well-being
within, the more tolerance for, interest in, and genuine caring we will have for others. So indeed, "May the whole team
be happy!"

Q I was recently passed up for a promotion, and a colleague got the job. How can I work with that disappointment and keep it from poisoning my relationship with my colleague, in front of whom I now feel humiliated?

A It is painful to go through what you are going through. I hope you can engender some compassion for yourself. At the same time, it can be useful to see that habitual reactions and distortions in thinking can make such situations even far more painful. Being passed over for a promotion doesn't mean you are a worthless person or that your colleague was purposely trying to hurt you. Quite impersonal factors might have (and usually do) go into decisions like that. The present moment situation also doesn't necessarily dictate what will happen in the future or how others regard you. Even as you relate to yourself with genuine compassion for the pain you feel, you can use mindfulness to look at and let go of the habits of mind that tend to make a bad situation so much worse. Try looking at the situation as one small piece of the much larger, richer picture of your life. Be open to people who remind you that you are smart, capable, and important to them.

CHAPTER 5

Communication and Connection

IN A CULTURE THAT VALUES INDIVIDUALISM, self-reliance, and the personal pursuit of happiness, it's easy to overlook the fact that we are interdependent beings. At every moment of every day, we're inextricably linked to those around us. The ability to connect with our colleagues—through skillful communication and other means—is paramount to being happy at work. What's more, there is a vital link between good communication, skillful self-expression, and integrity. How present you are, how able you are to manage your own emotional states—as well as complex and nuanced relationships—is essential to getting work done.

SKILLFUL SELF-EXPRESSION

S elf-expression does not require that we tell everyone what
we think of him or her at every opportunity. That would
qualify as self-indulgence, not skillful communication. Using
self-expression well means being truthful with ourselves and
knowing when, how, and with whom to share truthful information as an expression of personal integrity.

Allison, a public relations officer for a Fortune 500 company, comes up against this all the time. "Thankfully, at my job
I can speak up and say, 'Hey, what we're proposing to do is not
as honest or forthcoming as it needs to be.' I take this responsibility seriously not only out of respect for my own values, but
also in taking responsibility for information we share with the
public. I have some latitude to push back when it's the right
thing to do." Allison is constantly surprised by how subjective
integrity is. "Different people define it in different ways. A
major corporation is going to talk about integrity differently
from a practicing Buddhist."

It's important to know that you have a voice. It's important
to listen if you are a boss. Integrity means speaking up—
if only to yourself. That may sound like an oxymoron but
it isn't.

We often lie to ourselves about our true feelings. We all
too often suppress the dangerous knowledge of what we truly
think and feel and want from ourselves. We believe that if we
tell ourselves the scary truth, we will be forced to explode our
lives; that the force of confessing what we really believe will

wreak anarchy on the status quo. This paranoia about being fully honest fosters unhappiness in the workplace. But how can we be fully honest without blasting the boss, or causing disorder?

My friend Paul told me this story: "I started as a coordinator in a production company, and I'd write up documentary pitches and send them to an executive producer (EP) I trusted, hoping to get my big break, but mostly nothing happened with the pitches. Then one of the ideas I gave to an EP was green-lit (commissioned) by a broadcaster. That's a big deal! But the EP never told me. I found out my pitch was in production from another executive at the company during a meeting, and when I mentioned that I pitched that story, I was told that I had nothing to do with it. I was furious. I felt betrayed, heartbroken, and small. That's where my meditation practice saved me. Instead of acting out of my explosive feelings, I sat with the emotions for a couple of days. I sat until I could clearly summarize what happened in a one-sentence email to the EP I trusted with the idea, "I pitched my idea to you, it was green-lit, and you didn't credit me." And then I added a sentence that would not be possible without the days of letting the emotions pass through me, 'I didn't think you would do that.'

"In thinking about this, I rediscovered the reason I sent the pitch to the EP in the first place: I trusted him. I was seeing with a more spacious perspective again. Sure enough, the EP stopped by my desk by the end of the day; he explained it was all a big misunderstanding, offered me a job as an associate producer, got me the credit on the film, and gave me every reason to restore my trust in him in the years that followed. It was from my meditation practice of letting the painful emotions be felt in the body, and holding back from acting out of them, that allowed me to recognize that what looked like one of the most painful situations of my career was actually the big break I was looking for."

How we communicate has everything to do with maintaining well-being and harmony at work. People may look at it differently, but it's there. "Ethical communication is by far the most challenging aspect of working with others," former police officer Cheri Maples finds.

Stealth Meditation

a situation of potential conflict, let compassion guide you. What would you want someone to say to you if they were upset with you? What would you want hear if you knew there were two legitimate sides of the story?

Brenda, a technical assistant at a bio-med company, finds that being mindful of her own inner responses during conversations with colleagues is her most effective tool for good communication ". . . It takes concerted mental awareness not to slip into the clipped, irritated, fine-just-forget-it mode that might seem easiest but will actually shut down communication. When I can stay aware of what's going on inside me, I can keep the channels open toward others instead of reacting out of annoyance. It's a challenge at work, but when I can do it, it protects the colleague relationship."

We can use three criteria to help with skillful communication—at work and everywhere else. First, is the information *true?* Truthfulness must be the bottom line when considering what and what not to say. If we're being half-honest, we compromise our integrity and risk our colleagues losing trust in us and what we have to say. If we've determined that the information is true, the next question to ask ourselves is whether this communication—at this moment—will be *useful.* It's important to be sensitive to context, timing, and the profile of your listener before saying things that could do damage. I knew a spiritual teacher who used to say, "You must speak to a person's listening," meaning that skillful communication requires awareness of whom you're talking to and the degree of their openness to new information. Finally, it is wise to consider whether what you're about to say will be done in a *kind* way—as in polite, nonaggressive, nonconfrontational. The issue of kindness may point to the nature of the information itself or to your intention in sharing it. Do you have a secret agenda? Is this secret agenda constructive or destructive? Do you feel "clean" in this communication, or is it tainted by competition, manipulation, or malice? When communication fails to meet these criteria—of being true, necessary, and kind—we're wise to hold our tongue until we've vetted what we have to say.

WHAT DO WE WANT?

It is easy to forget in an action-oriented culture such as ours that everything we say and do is preceded by thoughts and intentions. Mindfulness of our inner world at work enables us to communicate and connect more skillfully with others through compassion and clarity of purpose.

Nicholas, a newly minted seventh-grade teacher at an inner-city school, discovered the importance of right intention during his first week on the job. "I was nervous that the kids would see me as a wuss. Truthfully, I was scared to death. It was thirty-five of them against me; that's how I saw it. Most of these kids came from low-income, broken homes and needed me to be in charge. Even though I wanted them to like me, I was more focused on getting them to respect me. When a couple of them got rowdy during class, I came down on them hard. Instead of quieting down and cooperating, the bad behavior just got worse.

"This went on for a couple of weeks. Whenever there was trouble in class, my response was to yell and throw my weight around in order to—I thought—earn their respect. But it didn't work. We kept butting heads. Finally, I asked the worst of the troublemakers to stay after class and talk. I wanted to understand what was happening. The first thing they wanted to know was why I had such a big chip on my shoulder. At first I denied it, but they were right. I did have a chip on my shoulder! It came from being scared—although I didn't need to tell them that! They could "read" that my disciplinarian thing was coming from insecurity and did what kids always do when they pick up on that: They acted out.

"My real intention was to be a good teacher, but my fear of being disrespected was overshadowing what lay beneath. As soon as I realized this, my attitude started to change. I started listening to the kids more and letting down my defensive wall. I realized that fear had been dominating my approach, and once I realized that, I could be more mindful of my tendency to control them through the power of authority. Now I try to connect with them, and it is completely different. We get along so much better now, and the bad behavior has mostly subsided. I'm not trying to control them as much as I'm trying to *teach* them. That's a much more positive intention."

Skillful communication is a multilayered effort. At times, it's best to speak up; other times it's best to listen. Talking and listening are two distinct functions that affect conversation differently. This is a case in point used by Mudita Nisker and Dan Clurman of Communication Options in their communications training seminars. They have noted that many of us confuse talking and listening without considering which function would work best in a specific situation.

For example, Bob, a software engineer, had recently received approval to develop new software for his company's largest customer. Bob's first impulse was to persuade his quality control manager, George, to test his new program immediately, but George already had several projects ahead of Bob's. Hard as Bob tried to sell George on the benefits and potential profitability of his product, George remained unsympathetic to Bob's proposal. When Bob's frustration quieted down long enough for him to pay attention to what was happening, he realized that George wasn't going to be more receptive until Bob listened and explored George's concerns.

As it turned out, George was reluctant to proceed until he knew more about Bob's track record and whether his team had a history of success, because George could be putting his reputation on the line if he gave priority to Bob's project. Bob realized he had to provide evidence of his past success and listen more fully to George. When he did, he realized how significantly George's concerns about his reputation were influencing his decision. Only then could Bob take action toward giving George the assurance he needed. By learning to listen, Bob was able to communicate with George more effectively and get the green light for his project.

In order to improve communication, we must learn to be mindful of what would best achieve the goals of both parties. Listening to understand without agreeing or disagreeing can show how open you are to someone's ideas—and how open they can be to yours.

THE CULTURE OF DISPARAGEMENT

When we urge people to say what is true—simply, without judgment or embellishment—that doesn't mean being brash or inappropriate. Sensitivity and discernment are critical. Especially now, when the predominant culture in the West increasingly seems to be one of disparagement. In the same way that we are encouraged to see cynicism as strength and kindness as weakness, we are taught to feel better about ourselves by putting others down.

We live in a society where many people revel in seeing other people lose, be spurned, and fall into despair. According to professor Paul Gilbert of Derby University, we see this ethos mirrored in reality TV shows like *The Apprentice,* which he likens to Roman gladiatorial contests. "Supposing all the young people watching *The Apprentice* thought this was the way people did business, with all the back-stabbing and attacking each other," Professor Gilbert said during an interview with the newspaper the *Independent.* "Would you really want to live in a world where everyone did that?" Obviously not, yet there are many work environments that seem to be modeled on the blood sport of the Roman Coliseum. "So much is going on that is making people angry," Gilbert adds. "I think people feel a bit hopeless." Despairing as this sounds, there's a sober truth in what Gilbert is saying. In a culture of disparagement, pessimism is the prevailing order, and the law of the jungle too easily becomes our psychological model for work. In this paradigm, there are winners and losers and little belief in win-win situations. The gladiatorial model of work presented by a show like *The Apprentice,* emphasizing power over compassion, disparagement over cooperation, and self-aggrandizement over team spirit, weakens connection with our co-workers and makes skillful communication less likely.

It is notable when we find colleagues or even a boss who want to see us succeed. Caroline relates, "When I was in my

Stealth Meditation

For an upcoming one-on-one conversation, resolve to listen more and speak less.

twenties, I worked for some time as a waitress in a health food restaurant. One day a customer ordered a soy cappuccino, which I had to make myself—all waitstaff did this. On the best days, it was not a quick process and perhaps I was not being particularly speedy that day. After some time, the customer came to the back and asked about the drink she'd ordered. I snapped at her, saying, 'It does take some time to make, you know!'

"My manager observed the interaction, her eyes widening as she looked at me. She said something like 'that was rude!' and I thought she was referring to the customer. So I said something like, 'I know! Can you believe these people?' And she said, 'No, I was referring to you.' I was genuinely taken aback. I was so sure I was right in this situation. After the customer got her coffee, the manager asked if she could speak to me in her office. So I got myself all into a huff and ready for a fight, ready maybe even to quit or get fired, since I was so completely sure of myself in this situation and was feeling quite wronged now somehow.

"I walked in and sat down, and instead of reprimanding me, my manager began by complimenting me with utmost sincerity on my work at the restaurant, my general character, et cetera. She was soft, open, genuine, and far from accusatory. I completely deflated. I was now unarmed—taken by surprise by her genuine kindness. I simply could not fight with her after that and I just kind of melted. When she finally did get around to talking to me about my behavior earlier, I could actually hear her and agreed I could have handled it differently.

"That she took the time to see my humanity and was able to communicate that to me made all the difference in our interaction and in the outcome. I was also quite different with her after that day. I no longer saw her as 'the other,' 'the boss,' but as a fellow human being just trying to do her job as best as she could."

APPRECIATIVE INQUIRY

Appreciative inquiry is a method that focuses on increasing what an organization does well rather than eliminating what it does badly. It is based on the philosophy that whatever you want more of already exists in any system (individual, organization, community). The traditional approach to organizational development focuses on problem solving—the "what's wrong and how can I fix it?" method. Appreciative inquiry works to identify what is working and then determine how to remember, reinforce, and amplify the positive aspects that support organizational health and well-being.

This model rests on the assumption that the questions we ask tend to focus our attention in a particular direction. It assumes that every organization and every person in the organization has positive aspects that can be built on. It asks questions like "What is already working well?" and "How can we reinforce and build on what you are currently doing?"

Ellen Carton, an organizational development consultant, describes her experience using this model: "Typically, I am asked to intervene to help solve a problem like low staff morale. Prior to my engagement with appreciative inquiry, my approach would include conducting interviews with individuals—asking questions like 'what's going on here; what is the problem? What is morale like? Why do you think morale is low? Can you give me examples of low morale?' And on and on. I would indeed learn much about low morale. Additionally, after several hours of questioning, my own energy would be depleted and I would be somewhat discouraged. And that was just the starting point of the process! While I learned about the current negative situation, I did not discover any potential solutions that might already exist in that system.

"After learning about appreciative inquiry, my approach—and results—took a dramatic turn for the better. I would facilitate conversations by asking staff to tell stories about a time when morale was high in the past and learn about the circumstances that supported the positive experience. It wasn't always easy—people often have the tendency to want to focus on the negative, and it's important to allow them to 'vent.' But with a little probing (and a healthy dose of patience), people do remember those positive moments and are then able to experience hope for the future.

"The impact of these conversations was profound—I was able to reflect back to the organization that they indeed have experiences of high morale in their organizational DNA—even if these experiences are the exception rather than the norm. From that point, we were able to amplify and reinforce those positive moments and build toward a better future. Not incidentally, my own energy and enthusiasm was heightened by these positive, life-affirming conversations."

Ellen goes on to say, "My discovery of appreciative inquiry coincided with my nascent spiritual practice, and it was easy to see how focusing on life-affirming systems dovetailed perfectly with my personal evolution from looking at the world in a highly pessimistic way to finding more peace and joy through practicing yoga and meditation."

Appreciative inquiry, if misunderstood, can seem like squishy happy talk. But take the case of GTE Information Systems. Appreciative inquiry began at GTE in the mid-1990s as a pilot program started in order to see what would happen if employees were trained in the basics of appreciative inquiry and then gathered positive data from throughout the organization. Each employee conducted interviews to find positive examples of what was working well. They found stories of exceptional customer service, constructive work relationships, and encouraging management. They called this "the Positive Change Network."

Stealth Meditation

At the beginning of a meeting, silently offer the phrases of lovingkindness to all others at the meeting.

Soon the Positive Change Network drew thousands of GTE employees. Over 10,000 innovations were attributed to the appreciative inquiry process, earning GTE the 1997 American Society for Training & Development award for best organizational change program in the country.

GOSSIP

It is important to mention the role of gossip in workplace communication. Gossip is nearly impossible for people in groups, at work and elsewhere, to resist. The reason for this is fascinating. Most of us don't realize that human language evolved in order for us to be able to gossip. Our early ancestors used gossip to protect the group from traitors, cheaters, liars, and thieves. Once we could talk, we could tell one another stories, especially stories about other people. We could watch one another's backs and also bite them; we could gossip as a social control instead of taking physical action. In other words, rather than beat somebody up we could simply ruin their reputation. Our brains have evolved to pay stories forward. Next time someone tells you a juicy piece of gossip, notice how hard it is not to repeat it. We're compelled to turn our relationships in groups into perpetual games of telephone. But gossip can cause devastation, since it is, by definition, nearly always negative.

Jesse's story illustrates how mindfulness can stop the cycle of gossip. "A few years ago, I needed to leave my job as an executive assistant for an extended period of time. My boss, a middle-aged man, hired a temp, a young woman, in the interim. When I returned, it was obvious that my boss and the temp were having an affair, which continued after the temp left the organization. My boss and I never had an open conversation about what he was doing, but I was able to clearly set the boundary that I would not cover for him with his wife or anyone else.

"I also made the decision that I would not share my knowledge of the affair with anyone at our organization—it was not their business. It was a painful situation that caused a lot of hurt for many people over years, but I was able to feel good about not gossiping and not enabling the situation when I confronted circumstances where it would have been easy to do either. That became my safe refuge through that situation."

It is remarkable how differently we can relate to others during conflict or turmoil when we learn to respond from a place of open awareness. To say that which is true and that which is useful, we need to pay attention. That is why it is so important that we learn to communicate with one another on an empathic level.

PAYING ATTENTION

Gina, a photographer and yoga teacher in New York, talked to me about the relationship between attention and mindful speech. "I have to be aware of how I interact with other people—especially when a challenge occurs," she says. "So much of what we do now is behind the literal and figurative screen of a computer where it's easy to fire off a quick reply to a faceless email."

Gina practices taking a moment to ask herself what her true intention is in the situation. "Is it to retaliate or get back at someone? If I'm so angry that I want someone to receive their comeuppance, I ask myself why and remind myself that everyone just wants to be happy. When they're acting out, it's usually because they're suffering in some way. If I still see red, then I step away to give myself the space to respond as I would want to be responded to."

Having gone through several major losses in the past year, the end of a marriage, the death of her sister, Gina is "deeply aware" of the "understandable, heavy feelings" she's carrying and working to be extra careful about not taking this grief out on her colleagues or yoga students. "I did not want to carry that into my work life on a day-to-day basis," she admits. "What I found is that the moment I stop focusing on myself, only then can I become present and able to focus on others."

There are a few basic rules of mindful engagement we can learn in order to avoid the most common communication traps. The first is to use "I" language. Consider this situation where Maureen is frustrated with Cynthia, an employee who is repeatedly late in submitting her weekly expense statements for Maureen's approval. She says, "Cynthia, you never care enough about anybody else to just submit your expense statement on time." Unfortunately, Maureen's use of the word *you* is practically guaranteed to make Cynthia defensive and reduce the chance that she will listen effectively. And the use of the word *never* does not help the situation at all.

However, what if Maureen were to use "I" language in this conversation? "Cynthia, I feel frustrated when I don't receive your expense statement on time. I had been hoping to leave earlier on Friday to spend some time with my daughter." The difference in these statements is significant. In the first, Cynthia could easily perceive Maureen as attacking her. In the second statement, Maureen is simply expressing her feelings in a manner less likely to be felt as confrontational. Also, there's not much room for argument in the second version; Cynthia cannot credibly dispute Maureen's statement that she is frustrated. This leaves less chance of defensiveness and an increased chance that Cynthia will be able to hear what Maureen is saying.

Even though it might seem somewhat formulaic, the use of "I" language is a skill well worth practicing if what we actually want is dialogue and authentic communication. Picture yourself going to the movies with a friend. As you are leaving after the credits, your friend asserts, "That was the best movie ever made!" There is now not enough room in the universe for you to say, "I didn't like it." Your friend has just defined absolute truth, and there is no room for you to dispute it! Whereas, if she were to say, "I loved that movie," there is space to offer your own point of view: "I didn't like it all that much." That's the moment an exchange of ideas and real communication can happen, even as you disagree about the movie. Expressing something as our own view, rather than as irrefutable, fixed, universally acknowledged truth allows everyone to have a voice in the conversation, which is how genuine engagement occurs.

A second powerful factor in skillful communication is body awareness. Most of us are unaware that only a small percentage of what we communicate comes through the words we speak. In fact, one study showed that in face-to-face interactions, 55 percent of the emotional meaning of a message was expressed through facial, postural, and gestural means, 38 percent through the tone of voice, and only 7 percent through words.

What is more, we mirror each other emotionally as well as energetically. If two people are sitting in a room, the electromagnetic energy of one person's heart impacts the other person's, as measured on an EKG. When you begin to become aware of how your body sends messages without your knowing it, you gain insight into the responses of others toward you. Let's say your boss says something annoying to you in passing. Instantly, your sympathetic nervous system is aroused, your heart rate increases, your respiration rate shoots up, and the stress hormone cortisol is released into your bloodstream. Essentially, your body prepares to react. If you're not aware of your physical response, it's harder to gauge your verbal response (with body language that's screaming "attack").

Mindfulness of the body will help you communicate without unwanted emotional baggage. Take the time to unclench your hands, relax your jaw, catch your breath, step back a couple of feet—literally and figuratively—and pause, rather than act out with unskillful means. Relaxing under pressure opens up new responses and possibilities, so you can choose the best course of action and then change direction if appropriate.

And the third rule is, once again, remembering to listen. When we meet someone new, or encounter a familiar colleague, the temptation so often is to be self-preoccupied, "Do they like me? How much do they like me? Was that an impressive comment? Was that a stupid comment?" And to be distracted, "No one would believe how much I have to do. Let's see, if I do that section first, I might be able to skip the other one altogether, and . . ."

Leslie Booker, founder of the Urban Sangha Project, offers exercises in deep listening, where one person in a pair speaks and the other is instructed to listen without interrupting, or even getting distracted by formulating a response just then. She has brought this exercise to New York City public school teachers, social workers, advocates, therapists, and lawyers. Leslie writes, "You can feel the urgency and tension in the room dissipate in the first few minutes as people realize that they're not going to be interrupted, their thoughts are not going to get derailed because of someone else's agenda. People feel heard and validated."

Without some ability to really listen, we might hardly notice who is there in the room or on the call with us. Or we might be locked into automatic ways of reacting and not take the time to see other possibilities. Carol, an attorney, recounts, "Many years ago, I was negotiating a huge case, with something like 350 clients. As I was talking on the phone to opposing counsel, I must have been very aggressive. It was a woman on the phone call. She was actually a nice person, I liked her but that was lost to me in that moment. However,

I was handling it, she said something to me, I don't remember exactly what, but the impact of it was 'We don't have to do it this way.' That completely turned my style around. What I found as a result of that turning point was that in negotiating cases, I just always looked for the human connection with a person, irrespective of the differences on the matters at hand. You may not ultimately agree on the dollar amount or whatever, but you find a space of happiness in your dynamic with that person. I found out later that after I changed, many people began to consider me one of the strongest negotiators in the city."

The ability *not* to be distracted or driven by feelings or held hostage by hostile impulses is mastered through practicing these communication skills. Remember that mindfulness often runs counter to what old conditioning prompts us to do. Mindfulness helps to interrupt our reactive—fight-or-flight—conditioning and become aware of the full range of possible responses at our disposal. It helps us distinguish what actually is in our power and what is not.

Deb, who runs a small nonprofit, describes, "In my work, I often come across individuals who seem unable to simply answer a question. I'm no angel when it comes to scattered conversations in social settings. Sometimes the best laughs with friends are found in tangential topic hopping. But when a work proposal needs writing or a project launch is looming, there's nothing quite as frustrating as trying to figure

---

Stealth Meditation

As you begin or continue your mindfulness practice, use your new sensitivity to make connections with colleagues who share your values and challenges.

---

out how to extract a vital piece of information from someone who knows it. In the past, when a colleague confused the question or changed the conversation, it resulted in my not getting what I needed and then in my getting frustrated. Now that I meditate, I tend to hone in on the task at hand more easily. My strategy gradually evolved into simply asking the pertinent question again. The meditation helps me think differently about what 'being focused' means. It seems incredibly simple—ask what I need to ask until I'm heard—but it's a bold realization. Decluttering isn't just for organizing my drawers and cabinets. That is what meditating does for me. It declutters my mind, and it makes finding what I need in there easier."

The more emotional intelligence and care you invest in the quality of your communication, the less you will be misunderstood or inflict unintended discomfort; the more likely you are to be effective and connected to colleagues; and the more you will strengthen your capacity for mindfulness in general. Rather than fall into tit-for-tat volleys for power or "being right," we can remember that animosity and alienation are mitigated by awareness, and our communications can be enriched by compassion.

Tarikh Korula, a tech entrepreneur, comments, "I have a regular sitting meditation practice. It doesn't always feel productive, but the benefits can bloom unexpectedly. I've spent the last year with a cofounder starting a new business venture. Businesses are made or broken in the early days. The constant pressure is intense and disagreements are inevitable. Recently, we found ourselves at one of those inevitable impasses. Tensions were high we were firmly entrenched in our positions.

"The logic of my perspective seemed obvious, and he felt the same way about his. We had stopped listening to each other. Then, unexpectedly, the bud of something sprouted. The fact that we were just trying to work together and found ourselves arguing instead, struck me as funny. The insight came fast, and I blurted out that he seemed angry. 'Of course I'm angry!' he boomed. 'Why?' I asked. 'Because you're being a jerk!' he boomed again. 'Okay,' I laughed a little, 'Why am I being a jerk?' He restated his perspective, exasperated. But in that space, I had become curious about his perspective, so I just gently asked him to explain how I was being a jerk. He calmed down a bit and when he explained it, I realized I had painted him into a corner with a broad brush, unfairly. I realized I had been reacting to an old scar, and not one he had inflicted. All of this happened more quickly than words, but I was overcome with empathy at the predicament I had put my friend in. Instinctively, and without thinking about the words, I apologized sincerely. Just like that, the smoke in the room cleared. His voice lowered, his shoulders unwound, he leaned against a wall, and we were able to see each other as teammates again instead of foes.

"I meditate because of moments like this, because it creates a time-lapse pill for insight. It helps me grow into the partner I need to be for my endeavors to work and for my relationships to be more genuine."

THE REALM OF EMAIL

All of these suggestions about communication apply to email as well. "When you type an email, before you send it, sit back, take three deep breaths where you're not thinking about the email, then return to the email and reread it—not so much for the data but for the emotional impact it will have on the reader," Chade-Meng Tan of Google recommends. "Imagine being that reader and try to look at the impact it might have. Then change it accordingly and send it." You can also send that email to yourself first. There's something about the process of opening an email in your inbox that changes the way you read it—it really makes it *to you*—and allows for new eyes. It's also good for proofreading!

Jared Gottlieb, who initiated a weekly meditation session at *National Geographic* put it this way: "I've found that the more care I invest into the crafting of a message, the less I fixate on it once I've sent it." Whether sending a personal email or composing a company-wide memo, this is excellent counsel.

In order to understand the role of mindfulness in modes of communication where we are not getting immediate feedback from someone's gestures or facial expressions, compare and contrast these two stories:

A few years ago, one of Robert's clients was pressuring him hard for a product on an unreasonable timetable. Robert fired off a harsh email to the client—one of those impulsive, emotional responses involving lots of capital letters and exclamation points. He clicked Send, felt a few seconds of righteousness, and then the doubt began to engulf him. The client forwarded the email to Robert's boss and everyone else in the organization associated with the project. Years later, Robert still feels shame arise when he sees someone who was part of that email chain.

In comparison, Scott says, "I've always been a fairly thoughtful crafter of emails, which, particularly in the practice of law, can be very helpful. I have long refrained from replying too quickly when agitated by the content of an email and am inclined to pick up the phone if I think it would be challenging to convey the spirit of a message through text alone.

But it was only after many years of practicing mindfulness that I realized the larger extent of my reactivity, especially when replying to emails.

"One day I was replying to an email that had asked a question to which I had a solid response. The reply took up about a paragraph, was finely worded, and I felt pretty good about it, but had a subtle unease. I looked over the email again. It was tight and concise, and so I prepared to send it. Then, for some reason, I decided to sit for a few minutes and pay attention to that subtle unease. A few minutes later, I looked up at the email and something about the second sentence seemed a little unnecessary. I deleted it. The message still made good sense. I relaxed into the moment again. A few minutes later, the fourth sentence was removed. The third

Stealth Meditation

Before sending an important email, send it to yourself first. When you open it as the recipient, you'll take in the tone, implications, and omissions that you might otherwise miss when you're focused on composition.

sentence was shortened. Then it hit me that I was removing language that made sense, but really had been included so that I might feel better about what I had to say, to assuage my own discomfort at the information I had to convey. The lines I removed were gratuitous and probably would have seemed that way to the recipient—or would be a source of confusion.

"When all was said and done, my reply consisted of something along the lines of 'Yes, that works for me, too. Thanks.'"

Retrieving an email is possible, but confusing and never guaranteed. It's better to pause and work with mindfulness before going ahead and pressing Send, rather than frantically trying later to act in time to erase our mistakes and avert negative consequences. We don't always get there in time. And besides, not many platforms or styles or forms of communication give us an Undo button. Not much of life does, either.

TEAMWORK

Most human beings have contradictory impulses: We love connection and group interaction yet also crave privacy and autonomy. We long to be recognized for individual achievement while also being part of the group. We want encouragement, guidance, and support, while also needing to be left to figure things out in our own way. Indeed, one of our greatest challenges at work is learning to be part of a group without betraying our individual needs, to play well with others while also being true to ourselves.

There is plenty of research to support the fact that the number of good friends an employee has at work is related to how engaged and happy that employee is. But some may find too much engagement counterproductive, since being crammed into a room is not everyone's ideal model for generating new ideas. A student of mine who works in the magazine business spends fifty-plus hours a week in a forty-by-forty-foot space with her two dozen stressed out, frequently bickering colleagues and finds it nearly intolerable. "My boss's idea was twofold. First, give nobody privacy so that they can't waste time. Second, shove us all into one room so we feed off each other's energy and get more done. Let me tell you that neither of these precautionary steps has made a lick of difference. All it does is keep us tense—there's nowhere to escape!—looking over our shoulders, unable to hear our own thoughts. I absolutely hate it!"

Contrast this with the experience of an ER nurse who relishes her shared space. "It's like sorority row, but we have a blast!" she says. "This place is like a tinderbox, emergency after emergency. If we were all in little offices, we'd be much less efficient. The fact that our desks are in a tight space enables us to work as a team, like one body. It wouldn't really work any other way." When it comes to skillful communication and maximum cooperation, a happy workplace depends less on where the walls are placed and more on where employees place their attention. Especially in tight working quarters, it's important to be mindful of our colleagues' mental space and not dominate the environment with unhelpful chatter, nosiness, and interruptions. One study concluded that people whose work is constantly interrupted make 50 percent more mistakes and take twice as long to finish their tasks. The ability to work in close quarters and respect the needs of the people around us is imperative to a happy workplace.

While office layout may vary, we do know that some people are more creative when they have privacy and freedom from interruption. People in many fields are introverts who enjoy exchanging ideas but see themselves as independent and individualistic and are not joiners by nature. When it comes to creativity at work, for some of us, brainstorming doesn't work as well as being able to go off into our own nook or cranny and then later share ideas spawned in private. This seems to call for flexibility and honoring the individual's needs whenever possible.

Teamwork has become even more complicated in the Internet age. In many global companies, work teams are geographically dispersed all over the world, and these virtual teams work across physical and organizational boundaries through the use of technology. By most accounts, telecommuting and virtual teamwork offer both drawbacks and advantages to worker satisfaction. Information technology that allows us to shrink global distances, fax documents around the world in seconds, and send emails hurtling through cyberspace, can give a false sense of solidarity, as if connecting with people required nothing more than knowing each others' Twitter handle or finding the best video-conferencing equipment.

Face-to-face communication is still a reliably powerful way of building trust and bonds among colleagues. But the assumption that employees who regularly telecommute feel less attached to the organization they work for due to isolation and disconnection may not be true. As long as companies integrate face time into their employee relationships, it doesn't seem to hurt to be working from home in your pajamas, seeing your coworkers only a couple of times a week. It can be good for productivity and worker satisfaction. The same principle holds true for people who work in close proximity to one another, day in and day out. Creative autonomy, access to quiet, some degree of privacy, and respect for one another's physical and mental space are important factors for many people.

THE RIPPLE EFFECT

A shift in personal awareness has transpersonal consequences. Emotions are contagious and have a ripple effect on the work environment, sometimes in ways we don't see. A recent study at Baylor University showed that spending forty hours a week with a nasty coworker is detrimental not only to the employee but also to his or her spouse. What's more, the difficult colleague's rudeness may have a ripple effect that extends as far as the spouse's workplace, not only causing unhappiness for the family but ultimately affecting the spouse's job as well.

Whether in the same physical space or not, our connection to one another is profound. At work, this ripple effect is happening at every moment. With each email sent, each call ignored, every negative water cooler conversation; or, on better days, every pat on the back, supportive smile, or task undertaken to help others; with every action we take, we send love or suffering into the web that connects us. When we shift awareness to acknowledge this ripple effect, we can undergo a sea of change as human beings. We find ourselves filled with a new sense of responsibility toward the quality of our experience and its impact on others. The shift of awareness from "me" to "we" sets the stage for a whole new life at work.

EXERCISE: Reflection on Interdependence

This is a practice that can be done in any posture and focuses on our interdependence—how we all need one another to accomplish what we want in the world. Just be relaxed, be at ease. And see if you can begin to trace back all those people who have been involved in your work life. Maybe you had a teacher who instilled love of learning and a willingness to be adventurous. Maybe you had a parent who instilled confidence in your ability to try new things or explore new terrain. Maybe you've had a child who's opened you up to a sense of wonder and interest you've wanted to express at work. Let a sense of them, a recollection of them, come into the room with you.

What about the clothing that you're wearing? How many forms of life, how many people, how many beings have been involved in the growing of that fiber, creation of the cloth, transporting it, selling it? And the creation of the building in which you're sitting, or the stewards of the plots of land if you're outside. All the forms of life involved in the food that you've eaten today, the creatures in the earth. Who planted that seed and nurtured that crop? Who harvested, transported, and sold the food? Prepared the food?

You can see that none of us is actually independent, alone, or cut off, however alone we might sometimes feel. We are all a part of the greater fabric of life, this immense web of relationships and connections and influences and interdependence. We arrive at this moment in time borne by a sea, an ocean of conditions. If we look at a tree, we can see it as just a tree, or we can look at a tree and sense the soil and everything that affects the quality of that soil, which is nourishing the tree, and the rainfall and everything affecting the quality of that rainfall, and the sunlight, and the moonlight, and the quality of the air. Is the tree just a tree or the confluence of all these conditions coming together, moving, changing?

And so, too, we can see ourselves as part of a great network of those who have helped us, those who have challenged us, a part of the work life of so many (as consumers, as communicators), and relying on so many others for each element of our own work life. Each moment of our experience displays how we are each part of a bigger picture of life.

~~~~~

EXERCISE: Mindfulness of Speech

1. Write down an accusatory statement about something that happened to you at work and put it in the second person, for example: "You're a loser for not being able to do your job properly and screwing up the deadline." Begin to rephrase it in the first person, that is, positive "I" language. For example, "I spent three hours looking for that file and missed my deadline. How we can set up a system so that doesn't happen again?" (Avoid the pitfall of disguised "you" language, such as "I felt bad when I saw what a loser you are.")

   How does it feel to authentically state the incident in "I" language? What kind of atmosphere is created by each way of talking about the same incident?

2. Notice if you are in the habit of using words like *always*, and *never*, and if you tend to be global in offering critical

feedback rather than specific, like "You are always disappointing" rather than "I was disappointed when you were three hours late." The latter, of course, leaves room for improvement and collaboration in that it gives the recipient something specific to address and work to change.

~~~~~~~

EXERCISE: Deep Listening

First, choose a partner, either a colleague with whom you're close, or a friend even if not a coworker. Determine who will speak first and who will listen and choose a mutually interesting topic. Then, sit face-to-face with your partner, resting your eyes on the ground or closing them for a moment as you begin to connect with the other person. When you're ready, slowly open your eyes. The first speaker begins. The topic might be hopes or fears about work, creating a supportive community there, ways that he or she might make a contribution. Speakers are asked to speak genuinely about their thoughts or feelings. Allow five minutes to speak without interruption and to listen with an open heart.

The listener's job is to simply hold the space for their partner to speak. Not to judge, fix, or offer suggestions. In listening, they are not to have a response ready the moment it's their turn to speak. As the listener, their *only* job is to receive: to pay full attention to the words, body posture, and facial expressions of the speaker. When the five minutes are up, a bell is rung and the two partners sit in silence for one minute with their eyes closed. The instruction here is to just let what was said settle, to not think of how to respond, but to let the speaker's words be their own.

After one minute of silence and gratitude, the other partner has a chance to speak. Not to respond to what his or her partner has just said, or to say what they think the other wants to hear, but to really connect within themselves and to say what is meaningful on the topic from their point of view. When given these instructions, most people are surprised at what they actually say. What they had rehearsed in their minds is not typically what comes out of their mouths in the supportive atmosphere of deep listening.

Once you feel comfortable with deep listening, you can bring this skill with you to conferences, phone calls, meetings, and one-on-one encounters with colleagues, clients, adversaries, and staff. Really, anyone you choose. No one even needs to know you're doing it—it's your personal, quiet instrument of connection.

~~~~~~

EXERCISE: Appreciative Inquiry

The following is an appreciative inquiry protocol, for reflection, journaling, or conversation.

This is an exercise designed to develop an expanded view of how to approach problems. It's easy, when we are hyperfocused on what's wrong in a situation, to reinforce a negative culture and start slipping into a feeling of hopelessness. This exercise is an experiment in approaching problems from the other side—what's right about the strengths and resources we can bring to bear in meeting our challenges.

- Without being modest, what do you value most about yourself, your work, and your organization?

- What would you describe as being a high-point experience in your organization, a time when you were at your best, when you felt most alive and engaged?

- What are the core factors that give life to your organization, without which the organization would cease to exist?

- Imagine that you have awakened from a long sleep. Your ideal state has become reality. What do you see?

- What three wishes do you have to enhance the health and vitality of your organization?

~~~~~~~~

EXERCISE: Mindful Email

Sit for a few minutes feeling your breath. Then reflect that one or more human beings, all of whom wish to be happy, just as you do, will be receiving an email you've written. Recognize that emotional tone is hard to convey in an email, and if it is unclear what emotional context you intend in your message, you may be misunderstood. Compose your email. Put yourself in the recipients' shoes as you reread the email. Revise it if necessary. Take three breaths before you decide whether it is time or not to press Send.

Q & A

Q I find it challenging to be mindful when working with colleagues with whom most of the interaction is via email. How can I make these people feel more human and less abstract?

A One of the main challenges of remote working is our tendency to form and hold assumptions about one another. Without regular face-to-face contact, we can fall into a rigid or dismissive image of someone. A powerful reflection would be to remind ourselves that all beings want to be happy and to offer loving-kindness individually to those we interact with via email, to help remember they are people and not abstractions. In addition, there are practical ways to remember their multifaceted humanity, perhaps with a question about family or a query into nonwork-related interests.

Q In any workplace, everyone would like to feel heard. But at the same time, not every decision can be made by committee. How does one balance these two things?

A Clarity is a big help. First, identify the times when a decision resides with one person. If you are that person, mindfully consider if you are listening to each opinion and conveying that each person who speaks is being listened to. If you are contributing to a decision that will affect you but that you do not ultimately make, find an opportunity to respectfully contribute, knowing you won't always get the final word or your advice may not be taken. Then remember that you did all you were able to and that things are always changing.

Q What happens if I offer loving-kindness to a difficult teammate, but the person continues to behave in unacceptable or undesirable ways? Are there ways to respond firmly even as I continue to offer them loving-kindness?

A There are different aspects of any action we take—anything we do or say. One is the intention or motivation behind the action. Let's assume you are coming from a place of genuine loving-kindness toward this difficult person. The next aspect is the skillful or unskillful execution of the action. This is based on our assessment of the right and appropriate thing to do in a particular context, at a particular time. It's important to distinguish between motivation (the first aspect) and execution (the second). Often we combine and confuse motivation and execution. When we do, we think that if we're compassionate, we have a very narrow band of activity available to us. We can only be "nice" and say yes to everything. In reality, you might sincerely be coming from a compassionate place, but your best sense of the most skillful way to behave in a certain case is quite tough, even fierce. Responding firmly doesn't necessarily mean that your motive is unloving.

CHAPTER 6

Integrity

I NTEGRITY IS THE SIXTH PILLAR OF HAPPINESS in the workplace. From the Latin word for *whole* or *complete,* integrity in the context of work means preserving a sense of wholeness and honesty on the job, aligning our actions at work with our own core values and principles. Without a foundation of integrity, it's impossible to feel good about ourselves or to respect what we do for a living. When work conflicts with our sense of justice or goodness (or both), we're bound to feel discontented. When our ethics are compromised, or our character's called into question, we suffer in response. As poet Maya Angelou has pointed out, "I've learned that making a 'living' is not the same thing as making a life." To feel personal integrity at work, therefore, we must be able reconcile who we are as moral beings, and what we do on the job.

Still, it is not always easy to "be yourself" at work. Workplace priorities, goals, and politics frequently contradict our personal values and our style of operating in the world. As one of my students puts it, "The primary goal of the company I work for is making money in ways that feel in conflict with my meditation practice and life, and as an employee, my job is to accommodate and promote their goals."

Work itself often makes conflicting demands on us to both compete fiercely and be cooperative, make tough decisions and be considerate, build profit without cutting corners, pursue rewards without becoming greedy. It can be challenging to find a moral compass to help us be decent, fair, and honorable. Our instincts to be authentic can come into conflict with the desire to protect our career, paycheck, reputation, or job. Yet success at any personal or societal cost is the opposite of real happiness.

In sticky situations, while working as a law enforcement officer, Cheri Maples would ask herself, what would Buddha do in *this* situation? "It sounds corny," Cheri says. "But there really is something to stopping in the middle of an ethical dilemma and pondering that simple statement, whatever spiritual teacher you admire. Thinking about ethical precepts or mindfulness trainings helps me to respond in a considered way."

Vietnamese Zen master Thich Nhat Hanh, Cheri's meditation teacher, describes these precepts as including: cultivating compassion to learn the ways of protecting . . . people, animals, and plants; becoming aware of the suffering caused by exploitation, social injustice, stealing, and oppression; cultivating loving speech and deep listening in order to bring joy and happiness to others. That's the ethical framework that Cheri attempted bring to her job, every day. "When I do something that violates my own ethics, I realize how it makes me feel afterward. My goal is to be a kind, loving person to myself and those with whom I work." When Cheri first made the switch from high school teacher to cop, she confided to one of Thich Nhat Hanh's senior students, a Buddhist nun, that she couldn't reconcile carrying a gun with the precept of nonviolence. "Who else would we want to have carry a gun but somebody who would carry it mindfully?" the nun asked her.

There's a story Cheri tells about the first time she saw the effect of mindfulness in action on the job. She was a patrol officer at the time, responding to a domestic call. A divorced father was refusing to hand his young daughter over to his ex-wife after a weekend visit. When Cheri interceded, he threatened her. Ordinarily, she would have slapped handcuffs on the guy and hauled him off to jail. But she had just sat her first retreat with Thich Nhat Hanh, and the experience "had broken open my heart," she says. She persuaded the father to release his daughter and then, instead of arresting him, spoke to him directly from her heart. Within minutes, he was in tears.

"Here I am, five foot three inches tall, with a gun belt strapped to my waist, and this six-foot-three man is bawling like a baby in my arms," she recalls. "I violated every tenet of my tactical training in that scenario." But a few days later, when she ran into the man in a local shop, he swept her up in a bear hug and exclaimed, "Thank you for saving my life!"

It doesn't matter if you're a cop, a businessperson, or a customer service phone representative, ethical behavior stems from having an open heart and treating others as human beings rather than criminals, competition, or the hundredth complaint call of the day. By remembering that ethical behavior is personal and emphasizing people over procedure, we're able to turn any job into an opportunity for wisdom and love and maintain a positive intention. The clothing company L.L.Bean is known for their superior customer service. It's interesting to learn that this humanistic approach "originated with (the company's) 'Golden Rule' of treating customers like human beings." Intrigued by the company's claim, I asked a friend to contact L.L.Bean to test this guarantee. He reported that, amazingly, "an actual person took my call in about thirty seconds, introduced herself personally, and walked me through the online ordering process patiently—which rarely happens—and *cheerfully*, which never does!"

INTENTION

Intention is considered to be the bottom line when gauging our actions. Positive intention is held as a prerequisite to skillful behavior. Take the question of competition, for instance. Competition arising from positive intention—to profit and excel without doing harm to others—is qualitatively different from the kind of cutthroat, deceitful, dog-eat-dog competitiveness that can characterize a workplace. It is only when the desire to win morphs into "hypercompetitiveness, moving against others" in one psychologist's words that competition becomes destructive.

Intention is not just about will—or about resolutions we make on New Year's Eve with shaky hope in our hearts. It's also about our overall everyday vision, what we long for, what we believe is possible for us. If we want to know the spirit of our activities, the emotional tone of our efforts, we have to look at our intentions. When I offer someone a gift, only my heart knows whether I'm doing it because I like the person or because I think, *Well, I'll just give her this and perhaps she'll give me what I want in return.* Each decision we make, each action we take, is born out of an intention. Sometimes our intentions are good but our delivery leaves something to be desired. A well-meaning friend of mine has a tendency to offer unsolicited opinions at work and elsewhere. Upon noticing a colleague's mistakes on a quarterly report—a report that had nothing to do with my friend's job—he informed the colleague of the mistake in a tone less respectful (and more nosy) than might have been necessary. Not surprisingly, his "help" fell on deaf ears, this colleague accusing my friend of "always needing to be right." My friend's intention did not match up with his delivery and created conflict in a situation where he wanted to be helpful. This caused him to do

Stealth Meditation

Set an intention for the day before beginning work. For example, "May I treat everyone today with respect, remembering each person wants to be happy as much as I do."

some soul-searching, to realize his tendency to mind other people's business, and to make a commitment to intrude less. Unfortunate as this episode was, he did manage to make the most of it by learning to keep his mouth shut until—and unless—someone requested his opinion.

The momentary urges that shape what we do are intentions, as are the convictions and aspirations we hold. When we stop before blurting out a nasty piece of gossip and ask ourselves, *Why would I divulge this?* we're tuning into our positive intention, our wish to not cause harm. By making an effort to notice our intentions with honesty and clarity, we gain a great deal of freedom. If we take the time to pay quiet attention, perhaps through meditation or contemplation, we may develop a completely different understanding of why we do the things we do. When we develop the habit of noticing our intentions, we have a much better compass with which to navigate our lives. We learn to cast a glance at our motivation before we speak or act, which frees us to live the life we want. And it frees us to see more clearly into what our actions mean to us and how we can genuinely manifest what we love and care about. Sometimes we need to just do the best we can in accord with our intentions and then trust in an unfolding we can't design or ordain. And pick ourselves up and start over if it seems we have failed.

Stealth Meditation

If you are feeling down or discouraged, consider helping someone at work. Science has identified a happiness-helping feedback loop. The more you help, the happier you can be.

DOING BETTER

Once you are aware of your values, you can see them in action—how they function and how circumstances can hijack your best intentions. In the beginning, you may notice this pattern long afterward—you will already have gotten angry for example, before you realize you've been simmering. Then you'll get better at catching yourself just a few minutes into the reaction, say as the anger is brewing. And then finally, you'll catch yourself just as the reaction is arising. Whenever in the process you catch yourself, instead of reacting from being off balance, center yourself in order to respond from a place of openness.

Trevor describes a situation in which he was teaching meditation to young people. "Just the other day, I taught a class for which I felt very prepared. I had thought through the lesson and was excited to try it out. I've been a teacher for nearly a decade, and I really felt confident going in. Well, it bombed. It was an epic failure from the very first minute, where everything and more that could go wrong went wrong.

"I see now that I didn't set up the instruction clearly enough. It was how to participate in a walking meditation exercise, so when I said go, all hell broke loose. Everyone was talking, walking past and around one another, walking slow or very fast, basically not engaging in the crux of the exercise. As it spun out of control, my face flashed hot and my rage bubbled just under the surface; I did the best I could transitioning from one activity to the next.

"I felt my own meditation practice helped, even in the face of that failure. First, I noticed that I was angry right away, and didn't lash out at the students for not performing as I had hoped they would. Second, even though I was angry, I just kept smiling because I wanted to remind myself that teaching, like everything else in life, rarely goes as we planned, and it can be funny rather than agonizing. Third and finally, because I didn't let the anger define the experience, I quickly sought out feedback to reconsider what happened and why. Earlier in my teaching career, I would have sulked for days, blaming the kids and myself, but with the help of mindfulness, I acknowledged the failure without letting it define me as a person or a teacher, and tried to learn something from the experience. I simply thought "That class bombed. Okay. Now let's get ready for the next one."

It is interesting to reflect on what we want most right now—to be seen as right or to be helpful? We can look at our motivation at any moment, and we can also notice whether we are counting on a shared motivation within a group of colleagues. Because I am acquainted with several scientists researching the effects of meditation—on the brain, on the immune system, on genetic expression—I have been privileged to attend sessions where one scientist will present his or her most recent research findings to scientists at other labs or universities. Once they finish, there is usually a pause, and then the questioning begins. The questions are often sharp, precise, and demanding. The underlying, unspoken ethic is that all are looking for the truth in a situation, that no one is acting from a selfish agenda or bad motive, and that this is how science works best—as a precise, exacting analysis of what is known now to open the door to what might yet be discovered.

Sometimes I would be there listening to those sessions and reflect on the trust involved. I imagine it must be awfully difficult for the presenting scientist to sit there, fielding those intense questions, possibly thinking *Why are you asking these questions? Are you trying to discredit my research because you are after my grant money? Are you resentful because I got to give that lecture and you didn't?* Instead, there seems to be a community, in the best sense of the word, of people seeking the resolution of a dilemma, a problem, a possibility. There is congruence and strong intellectual rigor and devotion to the truth.

MORAL DISTRESS

When the demands of fitting into a workplace—or of performing the job itself—conflict with an employee's ethics, it leads to moral distress. The pain of moral distress ranges from minor confusion and hesitation to a piercing sense of a soul wound. In a workshop I led years ago, a woman wept bitterly, talking about working for an insurance company and, as a matter of policy, having to turn down requests for reimbursement for the cost of wigs for women with cancer who'd had chemotherapy. A firefighter I know loved the men at his firehouse like brothers, but couldn't bear the way women and ethnic minorities were commonly derided in conversation.

One student of mine worked at a sushi restaurant where she was told to lie—or omit the truth—to customers who queried her about the freshness of the food, which wasn't always at its freshest. Forced into an ethical corner, she opted for integrity. "I could have gotten away with it. It's not like the food was bad—it wasn't going to make anyone sick—but these were purists who wanted to know if the fish was caught *that* day. Often it wasn't, fresh though it may have been. I decided to tell them the truth. It wasn't worth compromising my integrity so the restaurant could sell a few extra meals." She found that when she was able to remember who she was as a person, rather than as a role in a job, she felt the flexibility to follow her moral compass.

Moral distress becomes even trickier when it is your responsibility to defend the company's integrity to the public. "It's my job to handle crisis management—to investigate the crisis within the company and uphold the corporate responsibility to explain the crisis to the public," explains Allison (the public relations officer we encountered in Chapter 5). "There are legal ramifications for what we can and cannot say, and ethical implications for what we do say, when millions of people are on social media asking questions, demanding information, and reporters from *The Wall Street Journal* and *The New York Times* all want details." Challenged to "take in all of the information" and figure out how to uphold her own integrity, and the integrity of the brand that she's representing, Allison struggles to walk the ethical tightrope between reputation management and full disclosure. "I have a responsibility to the public and to the truth," she says, as well as "to be respectful to our employees and our company." These competing moral interests often leave Allison exhausted.

What helps us deal skillfully with this kind of distress? First of all, we need to name it. We can then use mindfulness to look deeply into the common ways moral distress manifests for us (anxiety, anger, depression, etc.). The next time you are suffering distress, ask yourself a few key questions: Do you believe that you've made an error? If so, what can you do to make amends? Or, are you taking responsibility for activities outside your control? Take an honest moral inventory: Is there an area where you feel your integrity is being deeply challenged by your work environment? If these activities offend you morally, is it worth the suffering to stay in the job? Or are you being self-righteous and projecting judgment onto others unnecessarily? If we develop a more mindful relationship with our distress, we can better see if a moral injury, which strikes at our sense of who we are and who we feel we should be, is part of the cause. Then, we need to relate to ourselves with compassion. If we understand that this kind of distress is actually born of caring, we can evoke more compassion than judgment. Self-awareness and self-care are critical tools for dealing with our suffering.

In addition, we must work to relate to others with compassion. We needn't assume a moralistic stance or be self-righteous, but we can understand that many forces go into shaping someone's view of appropriate action. We need to articulate our own view in a way and in an arena that is safe for us. And we need a support system, whether it is our peers or people outside of the work environment, as we make our way through the process of evaluating how severe the injury is to our sense of values, and whether we can stay at the job.

And if we are confused about the ethical nature of our work, we need to pay attention to the severity and duration of that confusion. I've seen people in work situations where the concerns they were bringing up weren't easily described as right or wrong. But I remember one woman in particular who continually and anxiously questioned the ethical nature of her work (while she wasn't especially anxious about other parts of her life). She was thinking about her job all the time; it was really weighing on her. At one point I just said to her, "You know, if you're thinking about this all the time, it's taken over your life. Can you change that? If not, what is the cost of continuing to do that work? Can you see a way to integrate your values and ethics into your work, so that your life is seamless? If not, can you gauge whether staying in the job is worth the suffering you are experiencing?"

THE MORAL DEMANDS OF COMPASSIONATE HEALTH CARE

Doctors, nurses, social workers, clergy, and individuals in caretaking professions often find themselves in morally distressing positions concerning life and death. Recently a nurse working in end-of-life care told me how alienated she felt from many people at the institution that employed her because of their belief in preserving life at all costs. Interestingly enough, critical care workers commonly report more concerns about overtreatment than undertreatment, and acting against their conscience when caring for the terminally ill. Health-care workers' distress is often tied to the economics of the medical world. Scarce resources, conflicts of interest, and lack of support systems are among the most frequently cited causes for moral distress in medicine. Data show that two out of three nurses experience moral distress on a regular basis.

Moments of ethical confusion in health care require extreme sensitivity and mindfulness of personal moral parameters. Meditation and mindfulness practices foster sensitivity and compassion toward others as well as ourselves. Consider these three testimonials by health-care workers following a four-week meditation program:

Gretchen: "The colleagues that I work with in the emergency department who have participated and are willing and want to participate—I've noticed a real shift in how they're able to function day to day; to see extreme scenarios and overcome them and support one another. The shifts I've noticed in myself are the capacity to assess difficult situations with more stability and calmness and then to grow from them. When people die after a traumatic turn of events, often I see surgeons, ER doctors, and nurses walk away in frustration, throw their gloves off, and you can see a sort of defeated attitude. And I decided to implement a mindfulness pause. It's a way of stopping, recognizing the person in the bed is a human being, and just acknowledging and honoring them, in my own way, in silence. And it really made a difference after major traumatic events. We even have the families participate."

Sylvia: "One of the changes that I've noticed in myself is the ability to lead from a more grounded place. To make decisions from my gut, using my body cues to really sit with a decision and say, 'does that feel right in my body?' before I make a decision one way or the other."

Patrick: "As an oncology nurse, I've always strived to give compassionate care to patients and families and my colleagues and students, but when my working environment becomes emotional and distressing, I often lose sight of that priority. The shifts I've noticed in myself are the ability to pull back when I feel I'm losing my focus on compassionate care and to be more mindful in keeping those goals in the relationships, to nurture the patients and families, and to always be supportive and hopeful and encouraging to everyone that I interact with. I think what energizes me and keeps me resilient is the ability to look around and see colleagues who have this priority, too. If I'm feeling a little worn out or discouraged, I can look to my colleagues for support."

Mindfulness decreased moral distress in the work lives of these medical practitioners. Dealing with matters of life and death, they are better equipped to cope with complex ethical situations and the emotional intensity of their jobs. Relieved of internal confusion, they're better able to help others, be happy in their demanding work, and remain authentic with themselves and others.

AUTHENTICITY

It often appears that a sense of morality has been squeezed out of an organization's operating manual. Allison describes her personal sense of disconnection from her job. "My integrity is tested on a regular basis. Working around people with completely different conditioning is a major challenge. My background is in Buddhism and nonprofit work, so what I bring to the table as a human being is very different from that of my colleagues. I was raised to stand up for what I believe, though, so I don't really have a choice about being myself. Sure, I get in trouble sometimes," Allison says. "And I don't always get my way. But I still do my best to be authentic and speak my mind."

Authenticity is inextricably linked to happiness—on the job and off. It rests on a sense of belonging. Not just in the way we normally use the word *belonging*—as being part of a team effort at work or being accepted into a particular group—but also feeling centered, feeling at home in our body, in our own sense of values, in our own dignity. It is a kind of confidence that doesn't come from attainment, but from knowing that whatever our particular roles or talents or job descriptions, we are all part of a bigger picture of life, we each matter.

This seems to be a thread running through the life of Mae Jemison, physician, dancer, engineer, NASA astronaut, and the first African American woman to travel in space. When she was twelve, there were civil rights demonstrations near Jemison's neighborhood in Chicago. The mayor called in the National Guard, which marched through the mostly African

American neighborhood with rifles. Jemison watched, and describes her way of going beyond fear: "I reminded myself that I was as much a part of this United States as the guardsmen," she recalls.

I particularly like the juxtaposition of Jemison's assertion of belonging in her own country, with the next affinity she expressed. When the space shuttle *Endeavour* was launched in 1992, Mae Jemison fulfilled her dream of orbiting the earth. She said, "I felt like I belonged right there in space," she remembers. "I realized I would feel comfortable anywhere in the universe—because I belonged to and was a part of it, as much as any star, planet, asteroid, comet, or nebula."

This is a benefit of meditation I have experienced, and witnessed in countless others: If we feel increasingly connected to an innate sense of worth, we have that ineffable sense of belonging. Then our behavior is authentic, at home or at work, wherever we are.

Authenticity is a fundamental proclamation that *who we are* and *where we are* arises from an original authority that makes us decent, intelligent, and profoundly resourceful. When we remember that authenticity shares a root with authority, this gives us a clue about how to maintain integrity at work. In being true to ourselves, we stay mindful of our moral compass in potentially compromising situations, like Jesse, the executive assistant who refused to field phone calls for his philandering boss. This is vitally important. The sense of being

Stealth Meditation

When walking to a meeting or to lunch, feel your feet against the ground and the sense of your body moving through space. Do not text or take calls while doing this.

subjugated at work, of laboring for someone else leads to powerlessness and professional victimhood.

A highly educated thirty-two-year-old New Yorker named Rose Marquez learned this the hard way. Employed at a political consulting firm, Rose discovered soon after taking the job that "the philosophies that surround me on the job and on the meditation cushion are quite different." In Rose's workplace, the loudest, most underhanded man often wins. As a younger woman, she is often tempted to behave like her bullying coworkers in an organization that is rife with competition, subterfuge, and resentment. Colleagues warned Rose during her first year that they had firsthand knowledge of her manager sabotaging her team, and although this was hearsay, it did nothing to bolster Rose's confidence.

Her values also cause Rose some confusion, particularly where assertiveness and aggression are concerned. She wonders how to assert herself without slipping into less skillful behaviors—talking behind people's backs, secretly competing, being defensive—and how to be compassionate while maintaining professional ambition, in a company where compassionate behavior is not generally rewarded.

"Meditation has been a blessing in moments like these," Rose says. "It has helped me work with the hurt and anger that inevitably arise, and it has given me the mental space to enjoy the many delights that exist beyond and within the workday."

In working environments like Rose's where the payoff for being greedy and grasping appears to be professional advancement, mindfulness is a powerful antidote to self-betrayal.

Far from being a black-and-white decision—to be "good" or "bad"—the choice of authenticity over "selling out" happens moment to moment and case by case.

Often, the "bad" choices being offered lead workers into ethical gray zones that are neither horrendous nor ideal, yet compromise their happiness nevertheless. A product designer named Brian is a case in point. Brian was hired by his company to create new products—or so he thought. After taking the job, his boss asked Brian to start copying other people's work, doing knockoffs of more successful products. "At first, this seemed like just the worst thing ever," Brian says. "I thought I was getting hired to come up with my own designs and improve existing ones. But really I was hired to knock off the merchandise of our competitors. No one at my company is really interested in breaking new ground because they don't want to risk failure. Since they don't want to risk failing, my integrity is compromised. I'm just supposed to keep copying stuff. And that doesn't feel good."

It feels better than unemployment, however, so Brian feels stuck. His work fosters ennui and self-doubt. Trudging day in and day out to jobs that don't fulfill us—but put food on the table—can lead to lives of what Thoreau called "quiet desperation." Brian questions his authenticity on a weekly basis while taking home his paycheck and keeping his ear to the ground for a better job. He tries not to blame himself for a less than perfect career, knowing that his core intention is a positive one—to create his own designs, which he'll be able to do once he finds a position where his talents are appreciated.

How we relate to the very sense of feeling stuck forms the path to finding a resolution to it. Even though it can be painful, being sensitive to our conflicts and dilemmas is part of the process of open awareness. That level of questioning has the power to open up deep learning about who we are and what we care about in whatever circumstance we are in. What's important is that we stay mindful of the vast array of thoughts and feelings we are having, and not identify with any story as permanent or final, such as "I'm a loser," "This is how it is going to be forever," "No way out of this!"

When we step away from the seductive influence of those stories, awareness empowers us and change happens more readily. When we hide out in stories about our situations, we lose energy for new perspectives or creating change. If we can keep paying attention to what we're feeling, even though it's uncomfortable, we continue to actively discover ways to integrate our inner concerns with our outer circumstances, even if the resolution does turn out to be letting go of a project or leaving a job.

Matt describes his ongoing experience of working toward such integration: "I began meditating because I was having a crisis in many areas of my life including my writing. I wasn't really that crazy about the last novel I'd written. It was kind of depressing and dovetailed with some things about myself and my behavior that I was struggling with. At the same time, I was also reading books and attending lectures on values like compassion and acceptance and loving-kindness and peace and ethical behavior.

"Right around then I started to write about soldiers and veterans of our wars in Iraq and Afghanistan. I began to meet with combat veterans and learn about the violence and trauma they both perpetrated and were exposed to. So in addition to the expected problem of being a lifelong civilian who wanted to write authentically about war but was ignorant about it, there was this other problem: How was I going to write about violence and terror, about the coarsening of emotions and the desensitization to the value of life that many soldiers were describing, while also moving in my meditation practice and my life toward greater compassion, peace, love, and morality? The answer is coming to me slowly. What I have seen so far is that choosing to be a civilian witness to war, choosing to devote some of my life and work to dwelling on the destruction that warfare causes to people, animals, plants, communities, is an opportunity to become a deeper student of the truth. Sharpness of tooth and claw is part of being an animal, and if I shun or turn away from this aspect of human nature, I am shunning or turning away from part of my own nature. What to do with this—and the stories I am hearing now from soldiers—is my ongoing challenge."

WHAT IS OUR WORK?

On the job, realization of what matters can come at the least expected moments. Being reminded of our humanity—our personal contribution to the role we're playing at

work—can suddenly return a sense of authenticity, even gratitude, to our life on the job. At the end of a long shift, a car
service driver had an epiphany like this when he was called
to pick up a customer at her home. He honked the horn and
she didn't come out. It was his last shift of the day, and he
thought about just driving away but walked up to the door
and knocked instead. After a long pause, the door opened
and a small woman in her nineties stood before him "looking
like somebody out of a 1940s movie," he said. By her side was
a small nylon suitcase. The apartment looked as if no one had
lived in it for years. "Would you carry my bag out to the car?"
she asked. He took the suitcase to the cab and then returned
to assist the woman. "She kept thanking me for my kindness.
'It's nothing,' I told her. 'I just try to treat my passengers the
way I would want my mother to be treated.'"

When they got in the cab, she gave him the address and
then asked if he could drive through downtown. He told her
it wasn't the shortest way. "Oh, I don't mind," she said. "I'm
in no hurry. I'm on my way to a hospice." He looked in the
rearview mirror. "I don't have any family left," she continued
in a soft voice. "The doctor says I don't have very long." He
quietly reached over and shut off the meter. For the next two
hours, they drove through the city. She showed him the building where she had once worked as an elevator operator. They
drove through the neighborhood where she and her husband
had lived when they were newlyweds.

Finally, the woman told him she was tired. They drove in
silence to the address she had given him. Two orderlies came

out. The driver opened the trunk and took the small suitcase to the door. The woman was already seated in a wheelchair. "How much do I owe you?" she asked, reaching into her purse. He told her she owed him nothing, then he bent and gave her a hug. She held on to him tightly. "You gave an old woman a little moment of joy," she said. "Thank you." Afterward, the driver couldn't stop wondering what if that woman had gotten an angry driver or one who was impatient to end his shift? What if he had refused to take the run or had honked once then driven away? By being authentic on the job, he said he was left with the sense of "never having done anything more important in my life."

EXERCISE: Looking at Motivation

Being more in touch with our motivations or intentions will reveal a lot about the ethical dimension of our actions. Before a conversation, pause for a few moments to determine what you would most like to come out of it. Do you want most to be seen as right, or as helpful? Do you want to foster progress, or hinder it?

Also pause before sending an email, with the same reflection: What do I most want to see come from this communication? The other party to feel diminished or encouraged? Them to go away or increase their involvement in my project?

And do the same thing before a specific choice or decision— What do I most want to see as the outcome? Peace or excitement? Ease or stimulation?

You don't need to condemn what you see, or decide you'll always see the same thing inside yourself, like a fixed characteristic, but try to become more sensitive to what is motivating you in this moment before you speak or act.

~~~~~~~~

EXERCISE: Visceral Feeling of Yes or No

There are many reasons we say yes—obligation, enthusiasm, peer pressure among them—and many reasons we say no, including courage, timidity, and confusion. Before you are about to respond to someone with a yes or a no, spend a few moments looking within yourself to see if you can tell where your yes or no is coming from. Be aware of your body, especially places where you find you hold tension, maybe your neck, shoulders, or stomach. Check your mood, to see what feelings are guiding your response. Check your mind to see what story is predominant. For example, *I could never succeed at doing that* or *they asked me only because everyone else must have said no* or *I'm going to put my heart into it and do it the best I can.* Then offer a conscious response.

~~~~~~~

EXERCISE: Having an Adventure in Virtue

We tend to think of adventures in exotic terms—climbing a mountain, visiting an exotic land. We rarely, if ever, think of an adventure in virtue. See if you can resolve to take an extra step in ethics for two weeks. If you gossip more than you should, make a resolve not to talk about a third party. Instead of talking *about* someone, if you have something to say, say it *to* them. If you exaggerate, see if you can stay within the borders of the truth. If you take office supplies home from the office, leave them at your desk instead. Stay aware of what's happening in your mind the whole time. How does the changed behavior make you feel?

~~~~~~~

MEDITATION: On Forgiveness

This is a reflection that can be done in any posture, eyes open or closed, just be relaxed. Call to mind a difficult emotion you've felt recently, such as anger, jealousy, or fear. Notice how you feel about that emotion. Are you ashamed of it? Do you dislike yourself for it? Do you feel you should have been able to prevent it from arising? Do you consider yourself in some way bad or wrong for having this feeling?

Then see what happens if you substitute the word "painful" as a description, for words like, "bad," "wrong," "defective," or "terrible." In making that substitution, we can begin to recognize that this state of anger or fear or jealousy is a painful state, it's a state of suffering. So instead of seeing your anger and saying, "I'm bad," can you say, "I'm hurting"? Each time you take a challenging emotion and change your description in this way, see what happens to your relationship to that feeling.

Now take that emotion, the anger, the fear, the jealousy, and fill your mind with it in order to see what it feels like in your body. . . . Observe the various sensations—maybe it's a tightening in your chest or stiffening in your shoulders.

Notice how you feel about that emotion. Are you ashamed of feeling it? Resentful? Frightened? Or are you relating to yourself with some kindness and compassion as you feel that emotion?

Notice the effect on the sensations in your body if you are relating to that emotion as "bad and wrong and terrible." Do you tighten your shoulders further, as if to ward off what you are feeling? Do you hunch over, as if to hide it?

When you are being kinder to yourself, what happens in your body? Is there a gentleness, a softness surrounding the tension of the difficult emotion?

Now imagine someone you care about filled with that same emotion—jealousy, anger, fear. Notice what happens as you describe to yourself those states of emotion as bad, wrong, terrible, horrible, and what happens as you respond to them as states of pain or suffering in your friend.

You can reflect on the fact that we can't seem to control when these feelings arise. We didn't invite them, we didn't wish for them, but as internal habitual tendencies are sparked by external conditions, they arise, and we see our own fear, jealousy, hatred, and so on. We don't need to be overcome by them, defined by them, fall into them, act from them, but we're actually not able to prevent them from arising. This is just the nature of things, for ourselves and for others. We can commit ourselves to trying to see these emotions very quickly, to recognize their painful nature, to have compassion for ourselves, and to let go. We can commit ourselves to remembering that when someone else is acting badly the state that is likely motivating them, of anger or hatred or fear, is a painful state, and we can have compassion for them. Even as we may take strong action to try to change the situation, protect ourselves, or take care of someone else, our motive in doing so need not be a sense of disgust or aversion, but can be that recognition of the pain they are in.

Q & A

Q I'm in a helping profession, but I've lost confidence in my ability to genuinely be of help. How might I recapture that?

A When we are in a position of trying to help, we often need flexibility of perspective. Instead of wrestling with the immensity of a seemingly intractable problem, for example, we might need to focus on a small victory. A child's smile, a bit of generosity from a client who said they had nothing to give, solar panels put up on a house thanks to a jobs training program, or one more day of someone's sobriety. These concrete, immediate gains all count, and we overlook them too often.

Q Old feelings of fear and self-doubt keep coming up at work. They can be overwhelming. What is the best way to deal with that?

A It helps to see our thoughts and feelings for what they are—thoughts and feelings. They are not true facts. Thoughts and feelings are impermanent and conditioned. As we become more mindful and have a little more space from those thoughts and feelings, we realize it's natural that they arise—we have some very strong habits—but we don't have to buy into them. Sometimes it is useful to give them a name and a persona. You might get a visit from "the doubter," "Helen who hides in the corner." If so, we can be cordial, but clear. "I see you, Helen, and I understand why you came. You can either leave or just sit there quietly."

Q How do I understand my true intention for an important interaction?

A Take a few minutes to identify what you would like your outcome to be in certain situations—a presentation, a call, an email, or a meeting. It's not unusual to find ourselves already in the middle of an encounter with no idea of what we really wanted most when we began it. Before starting a meeting, for example, reflect on what you would most like it to result in. For example, you might arrange a meeting with your boss to talk about getting a raise (and getting a raise would be a good outcome!), but interlaced with that goal you might find a wish to be heard, a commitment to stop acting like a wimp, a desire to be acknowledged. That will be a window into your intentions.

Q I have a passion for making a difference in peoples' lives. Without this passion, my life would feel pretty meaningless. But sometimes I get so frustrated when I don't see the changes I hope for or feel my colleagues are receptive to my efforts. How can I cultivate equanimity without losing my passion?

A Equanimity doesn't mean indifference or not caring. It doesn't lead us to apathy, but to the ability to sustain our caring for others. The point of equanimity is not to lose one's heartfelt connection with what is going on around us. Rather, it means balancing that connection with a clear recognition of the way things are. So, for example, we see what we might be able to influence in another person or system, but also what we genuinely cannot control, no matter how much we'd like to. We also see how much things are constantly changing, and so we keep on making the effort without needing an immediate, gratifying result. Even in the midst of intense, devoted work, we can be served by seeing such truths clearly and remaining balanced.

Meaning

WHAT DOES WORK MEAN FOR YOU? Is it primarily a paycheck, a means to an end for survival's sake? Does it give you social status, a life apart from your home life that creates a sense of yourself in relationship to the larger world? Are you competitive, your sense of meaning derived from victory over others, excellence in your field, promotion up a hierarchy of rungs in your chosen profession? The meaning of work is essentially subjective, contextual, and fluid.

Some sense of meaning is vital to being happy at work. Most of us want to feel that what we do matters, somehow; that we do it with an open heart, an intention to connect with others, to improve something in this world, to be part of the solution, even in some minor way, rather than be a part of the problem.

FULFILLMENT

~~~~

With all the time we put into work, it seems fair to expect some fulfillment in return. Our satisfaction, as well as a sense of meaning, may arise from any number of directions. The tasks we perform may be significant to us if we're lucky enough to do what we love for a living. We can also simply find meaning in being gainfully employed and capable of supporting ourselves. The meaning of work may come from the relationships we enjoy in the workplace or from promoting goodness in the world. Finally, we may derive meaning from working with adversity on the job, using work as a spiritual practice to work "against the grain," freeing ourselves inwardly in less than ideal situations.

We tend to have varied orientations toward our work. Are we doing it for a position and a paycheck? Are we identifying our work as a profession? Are we passionate about what we're doing? Depending on our predominant sense of why we are working, the things that give us fulfillment will vary. In 1997, Amy Wrzesniewski at the University of Michigan and her collaborators released a study on the different ways in which we experience work, breaking it down into three categories:

As a job. As a career. As a calling.

If you work out of necessity at a job that you wouldn't choose, the financial rewards of the position might hold more appeal than anything else and have the greatest impact on whether you stay or go. Many people work for the money, and that's not necessarily a bad thing. There can be great moral satisfaction in earning your own way in the world, being self-reliant, gainfully dutiful. Working to support yourself is not to say that work can't also be pleasurable, whether or not you have the ideal job. But for people who work to live, rather than live to work, searching for meaning in the tasks you perform can seem superfluous, if not downright silly.

If you see your work as a profession, you may find satisfaction or pleasure in the work itself, but the promotions, reputation, and opportunities to further your career are part and parcel of the meaning of your job. Individual positions are often seen as stepping-stones to future glory, a defined goal in the hierarchy of your chosen field. Your status or power at work is likely to have an influence on your level of satisfaction. And if you see your work as a calling, if you do what you do because of passion—whether or not you're getting rich or furthering your reputation—the meaning of your work will be in the doing. Healing the sick, painting a canvas, being a public schoolteacher, may be enough in itself to make your work life meaningful. It's not surprising to learn that people who work from their passion, and earn a livable wage, report the greatest work satisfaction.

That passion can take root in us from many different sources. I remember sitting in the majestic, imposing courtroom of the U.S. Supreme Court watching my friend David Ferleger argue a case he had first filed at the Federal Courthouse in Pennsylvania two years out of law school. The case was *Haldeman v. Pennhurst State School and Hospital,* and contended that conditions in the state school were inhumane and dangerous and that developmentally disabled patients in the care of the state had a constitutional right to appropriate care and education. I knew that David's parents were Holocaust survivors and that part of his intense concern with people who were treated as less than equal came out of his personal background.

Sometimes a calling comes to us when we're not expecting it. Leslie Booker describes how one came to her. "I was doing event coordination for a New Age holistic center after leaving the fashion industry. I met everyone who was on the circuit, and my mentor, Stan Grier, would say to me almost weekly, 'You should really teach for the Lineage Project.' The Lineage Project is a nonprofit that brings awareness-based practices like yoga and meditation to incarcerated kids in New York City. 'Why? I hate teenagers and I don't teach yoga; why on earth would I ever work with them?' I'd reply. It sounded like the one thing I would never do with my life!

"Stan, however, was the most patient and persuasive human being I've ever had the privilege to know. After about a year, I found myself in a yoga teacher training, not with the intention of teaching, but simply to deepen my understanding of my body and of the practice. Within a few months of completing my teacher training, I was teaching alongside Stan at a secured juvenile facility in the South Bronx."

At that facility they worked with young women twelve to sixteen years old. As Leslie taught, and slowly watched the women learn to express vulnerability, comfort one another, and openly grieve instead of diverting that pain into rage, a lot fell into place for her, "That's where I really understood what I was meant to do."

Yet any job can be meaningful, or meaningless, depending on how we look at it. Most of us have known miserable "successful" people who resent their golden handcuffs, and delightful, compassionate, and insightful people who work at jobs we don't normally associate with a calling, like housekeepers and cabdrivers. That cliché about having informed discussions of the intricacies of government policy with Washington, DC, cabdrivers often turns out to be true! Meaning is in the eye of the beholder. We can be purposefully helpful and attentive in conventionally trivial jobs and blasé-ineffectual in potentially world-changing positions.

I was once meeting some friends in San Francisco in order to attend several days of lectures by the Dalai Lama. I arrived at our hotel at night, tired, only to be told by the desk clerk there were no nonsmoking rooms left, even though I had requested one, and had called again to confirm my need for it. I have asthma, and I knew there was no way I could sleep in a room where someone had recently smoked without getting quite sick.

Exhausted by now, I went to the hotel restaurant to find my friends, to tell them I was going to start calling other hotels to try to find a room. The waitress, filling water glasses at the table, saw my distress and asked what was wrong. When she heard my story, she immediately went to get her manager, in charge of food service. They were both so kind! Even though they weren't involved in room assignments, they promptly went to speak to the desk clerk. Before I knew it, a nonsmoking suite at the price of my original room opened up for me, complete with a fruit basket and an apology. The waitress and the food service manager didn't have to do any of that, but it made a very big difference to me that they did.

The question is: Why did they do it? Was it for the simple satisfaction of doing a good deed? We are inwardly rewarded by being generous; in fact, altruism is linked to elevated levels of dopamine in the brain. We feel better physically when we help others. Or did their help stem from empathy? I may have looked upset and their kindness stemmed from my nonverbal call for help. The mystery of human kindness can be baffling. It is also a key to finding meaning at work. These lovely food service employees stepped outside the box of their given roles to help a distressed stranger. They acted as fellow human beings rather than just employees, and this made their jobs more meaningful in that moment. I could see how relieved they were, too, when that nonsmoking room materialized! You have opportunities every day to step beyond your role at work and act like a whole human being, offer a helping hand, learn the skill outside your scope of work, allow yourself to be helped by others. This will make your work life more humane and deeply fulfilling.

In cases where your job does not easily align with meaningful purpose, it's still possible to use work as an opportunity for doing good. Maia Duerr, founder of the Liberation Life Project, talks about having a "liberation-based livelihood." Maia recommends remembering your core intention and shaping its expression to the real circumstances you find yourself working in. Let's say that your deepest intention in life is to be a healer but you're working at a supermarket. If you do your job using the right frame of mind and focus on your positive intention, it is possible to be the healer you want to be while directing customers and bagging canned goods. As a healer working in a food store, you can greet every customer with kindness and compassion and bring that healing energy to your job. When your intention at work is to manifest the creative, proactive, most helpful and loving aspects of who you are—and what you care about—you can transform the most tedious work into an opportunity to help others, become more aware, and learn a lot about yourself. Each morning before you go to work, you can set your intention for the day. Don't let it be simply task oriented, like, "I'm going to clean off my desk, finally!" or "After all this time, I'm going to reorganize those files!" but something bigger, and bolder like "I will try to treat everyone I encounter with respect" or "Even if I am very busy, I want to take the time to truly listen to anyone who approaches me" or "When I see myself slipping into judgment, I want to remind myself that everyone wants to be happy; we just all get misguided sometimes" or "Instead of smoking a cigarette or blowing up at colleagues, I'm going to find practical, better ways of dealing with stress." Knowing and perhaps purifying our deeper intentions for our work becomes the basis for sensing what will bring us fulfillment.

Stealth Meditation

Use doorways consciously. As you come upon that in-between space, feel your feet against the floor, your hand on the knob; touch the doorway you pass through.

Matt Hagebusch, owner of Peace Frog Carpet & Tile Cleaning, writes, "I returned to the States after five years living and teaching in Japan, jobless and with very little money. Other than a pizza delivery job, I was unable to find work. With hesitation, I got back into the carpet cleaning industry where I had worked when I was much younger.

"I tried to bring the practice of loving-kindness into every customer's home, and I made it an intention to connect with every person I met. I searched for commonalities to discuss, like their dog, a piece of artwork, or travel experiences. Connecting with customers, leaving them smiling and happy, was not only my specialty, it was my personal policy.

"One early morning I went into an Indian gentleman's home. He immediately started adding rooms to be cleaned that were not on his original order and seemed to expect me to clean them for free. He ordered me around like I was a disobedient child. Irritated, I told him that I would leave if he was going to be abusive. He wanted to speak to my boss, and I wanted to tell him to go jump in a lake! I decided to clean as fast as I could and get to my next job. I put in my ear buds, cranked up the music, and got to work.

"Keeping with my 'no customer left unhappy' policy I decided to try to find something we both could appreciate. I happened to be listening to music by Krishna Das, which is beautifully melodic Hindu chanting. I asked him if he could possibly tell me what the words mean in these songs. I handed him my iPod and watched his facial expression change from agitation to sweet reverie. Face beaming, he hurried into an adjoining room and closed the door behind him. He stayed behind the closed door for nearly thirty minutes. When he emerged, he was wiping tears from his eyes. He looked at me and said he was unhappy with his life and expressed his gratitude for reminding him of his long forgotten spiritual practice."

Setting your intention is important everywhere and certainly in fields devoted to consciousness. Gina, the photographer and yoga teacher quoted in Chapter 5, has made this part of her daily practice. "When we're feeling lonely, isolated, or overcome with the daily stress of living in a big city, where we can lose 'connectedness' to everyone around us and to ourselves, I try to remember that being kind to oneself is key. This kindness can then extend naturally to other people. What I have found helpful when encountering a student or coteacher who may be having an off day is to remember that we all want one basic thing and that is to be happy. What restores me is knowing that my practice not only makes me a happier person, but the happiness that comes from my practice extends outward to everyone. Doing my work in a grounded way helps me experience the world and the people around me as the gifts they are."

When we lose our right intention—the inner spark of motivation for the work we once may have loved—our work lives can sour and job performance flatten. While intention is cultivated from within, we cannot help but be affected by attitudes in the workplace. Research shows that supervisor mindfulness has significant impact on employee performance and well-being. When leaders and supervisors show higher levels of mindfulness, employees show greater well-being and higher performance—"with less emotional exhaustion and a more contented sense of their own work-life balance." Leaders who are fully present when interacting with their subordinates get a better understanding of their employees' needs, increasing support and creating a sense of interpersonal fairness.

When the intention of the boss is to make us "feel heard," we are prompted to be better workers. And better to *ourselves* while on the job. But of course, we can't determine how others will treat us.

Employers can assist people in finding personal and specific passion at work. "Helping employees identify their talents and skills, uncover their work and life values, and assess the environments and activities in which their values will be met while their talents are utilized is a boon to the workplace," says Tom Welch, president of Career Dimensions in Stuart, Florida. When employees devote their talents to projects and companies that support their values, the work tends to be meaningful to them. Imagine the kind of commitment companies could generate by helping employees find and apply their passions while they're still employed.

ASPIRATION

A ri is a talented industrial engineer and amateur bass player who never wanted to work a nine-to-five job. As a millennial—someone born between the late 1970s to the early 2000s—Ari sees work as an important part of his life, but not as his entire life. After graduating from college, which was funded with loans, Ari resisted the pressure to take a full-time job and accepted his parents' offer to pay for graduate school to study music and help him pay rent. It was a great experience while it lasted, and Ari was happy being a student and teaching music as well.

Then the recession hit. Music teacher positions were cut. Ari moved back in with his family, stopped paying off his student loans, and delayed finding whatever jobs were available. He was anguished over his uncertain future, withdrew from his friends, and felt a strong sense of having been betrayed by the promise of the American dream. He wasn't feeling sorry for himself; he was genuinely shocked when making a living turned out to be so much more demanding than he'd expected. "My parents raised me to expect opportunity," Ari says. "Isn't that what this country's supposed to be about?" Ari isn't lazy and he isn't a whiner. He feels he was misinformed and now finds himself unsure of how to proceed. Should he stick to his dream of teaching music? Should he backtrack and get a graduate degree (on his parents' dime) in industrial engineering, even though it isn't his passion? Should he grab his bass and hit the road, hoping to be discovered? Overwhelmed by choices, none of which seem clear or right, Ari feels trapped.

An educator and former executive named Srikumar Rao has worked to help people like Ari move beyond their suffering. Rao says, "People have the choice of deciding which emotional domain they occupy. Much of the time we occupy the domain which leads to stress and anger, and we don't recognize that we have a choice. So stop looking at employers to make you happy. Take charge of it yourself."

This begins with assuming responsibility for our own happiness. As one expert puts it, "I am self-employed regardless of who pays me." When we work using our greatest strengths, dedicated to something larger than ourselves, we are likely to feel the most fulfilled.

Stealth Meditation

Look for ways to acknowledge someone's accomplishments. For example, you might praise their promptness, diligence, or efforts to collaborate.

When we believe that we have no choice, viewing ourselves as objects being moved from one situation to the next, we lose feelings of autonomy and personal power. Although a job may not be perfect, we are choosing the work we do at least for the moment (except for those rare circumstances where coercion or forced servitude come into play). Mindful that we are not victims, we break the mental model of "work or die," the feeling of having no choice, and tap into the creative potential of our situation. This creative potential can be cultivated in the most unlikely places.

As psychologist Martin Seligman puts it, "It is difficult to feel satisfied with something you aren't very good at, so rather than spend time beating yourself up about it, take a long, hard look at the things at which you excel, and try to find a position that uses some of those skills, too."

If fulfillment at work is not possible, for whatever reason, and if it looks like it really won't change, we turn our attention to cultivating meaning elsewhere. We can work on that book that's been rattling around in our head or the Internet start-up idea or community service project. We can get up early and devote our time to something we care about. Taking positive action in the face of intractable dullness or lack of advancement possibilities or job insecurity or the boss that righteously annoys you teaches us that we can, in fact, be happy and less-than-ideally employed at the same time.

Sometimes our meaningful hobbies can lead to changes of career. This happened to a student of mine named Laura. While Laura was a student in a musical theater program, in preparation for a career in that field, she saw a lot of folks walking their dogs on the street and missed having a pet herself. To satisfy this nostalgia for home, she began walking dogs for extra cash while preparing for a life in the theater. She loved taking care of, and later training, animals so much that she decided to do it professionally. "Because it's not really a job to me," she says. "I get to build a relationship with my clients and their dogs that focuses on their beloved pets. I meet a lot of clients who rescue dogs from shelters, and if I can help an owner with a puppy who has leash aggression, then I am reaching my goal of keeping the dogs happy and healthy and in a good home for their full lifetime. And I make money doing it!"

Ambitious souls like Emily, a senior publicist at an advertising agency, thrive on adrenaline-fueled environments. "When my job is going full speed, that's when I feel fulfilled," she says with some embarrassment. "I like being superproductive. I'm not saying that I don't get stressed out and nervous sometimes. But I'd rather be challenged than bored. I enjoy feeling game. That's why people at the office know they can rely on me to give 100 percent to a project. They know they can trust me, and I find this trust very fulfilling." Emily is quick to add that without her daily meditation practice, she would not be able to tolerate the pressure. "I need to empty out," she says, referring to the silence of sitting practice. "It keeps me aligned. During the day, if things get too heavy, I can go to my office, shut the door, and sit with my eyes closed for ten minutes. There are high-pressure jobs to be done in the world and somebody's got to do them," she says with a smile. "That person would be me."

I AM NOT MY JOB

In an ambitious meritocracy such as ours, it's especially easy to identify excessively with our position, profession, or role. This is true whether you are a steel worker or a meditation teacher, a gardener or a fashion model. Especially in competitive environments, it is a constant practice not to confuse our true identity with our public persona, or to "believe our own PR" in professions requiring self-promotion. In New York City, strangers at parties will often ask one another, "What do you do?" as the opening salvo to getting acquainted, as opposed to "How are you?," "What do you love?," or "Where do you live?" Using the ancient philosophical distinction between "doing" cultures and "being" cultures, ours is one defined by doing.

This is not to say that what we do for a living doesn't affect our off-the-job quality of life. Certainly, work provides self-esteem off the job, a structure for the day, a purpose for getting up in the morning and going to do something. Work can offer friends, a social group to belong to, a sense of being a contributor, part of something with a bigger purpose that's valued by society. However, while work may give us these benefits, it is risky to make it our reason for being.

Many jobs do not provide the social status that our ego might wish to project in the world. In the professional pecking order, we may feel like peons. An office worker named Tracy struggles with this. "It's a huge challenge to *not* see myself as just a secretary," says Tracy. "The fact that my work life is full of nonchallenging tasks is also an ongoing struggle. Many times it appears to me that my boss looks down at me. I do my best to be of service at a job that was never a great fit, practically or spiritually, and try not to let personalities get in the way of what my fundamental job there is. But it's wearing me down."

Tracy's story is all too common. So what can you do when your job fails to give you the ego satisfaction you might like? How can you maintain your self-respect in subservient positions where others may treat you, condescendingly, as a functionary instead of a whole human being? This is where the rubber of spiritual practice meets the road. Like all conditions that disappoint us, push our buttons, or challenge the image we hold of ourselves, inferior jobs offer an excellent—if not always pleasant—opportunity to work with negative emotions, practice humility, and strengthen mindfulness of unhealthy attachments to status, competitiveness, appearance, greed, and so on. Regardless of how much you hate your job, you can always learn from your own responses and use the experience to wake up. This may seem like cold comfort, but in spiritual terms it could not be more beneficial. From a spiritual perspective, while it's lovely to get what we want, of course, it can be more beneficial, more self-strengthening, and more enlightening, *not* to get it, since challenge and loss have the power to reveal where we are deluding ourselves ("If only I got a promotion, I'd be a more worthy person!"), and shift our awareness to what is true; namely, that job titles, salary, impressive responsibilities, have nothing to do with who we really are. This inevitable gap between what we want and what we get, serves a vital function: to remind us of impermanence, directing our awareness toward what truly matters.

As the songwriter Leonard Cohen puts it in one of his songs, "There is a crack in everything/That's how the light gets in." In other words, when we experience dissatisfaction at work, which everyone does sooner or later, regardless of how impressive their job is, we can use our disappointment as fuel to wake up. So you thought that your job would solve all your problems? Big surprise! So you believed that job success and appreciation would render you forever secure, shore up all your self-doubts, your craving for esteem, and your faith in universal fairness? Hello! Waking up from our most cherished illusions is a vital step in spiritual maturity. Realizing that everything changes and nothing satisfies completely is comparable to no longer believing in Santa Claus, shocking at first but fortifying in the long run. Like intense disappointment on other fronts, such as family dynamics, romantic heartbreak, and the concerns of aging (which a friend of mine calls Miracle-Gro for your character defects!) letdowns at work may bring out the worst in us in order for us to heal and free ourselves of false expectations.

Mindfulness is the tool we use for forging this path. Realizing that our jobs are conditional and impermanent, like all relationships, we learn to perform these jobs well without losing ourselves to these temporary roles. Jessica, who works as a cocktail waitress while waiting for her break as an actress, has discovered that she can enjoy her work without it coloring her self-image or clouding her larger purpose. "I have always felt I could survive in this job as long as I maintain my own boundaries," Jessica explains. "I am happiest when I'm able to keep everything totally separate. This has always been my goal since waitressing was not what I wanted to do with my life. A lot of people I work with get really frustrated because they take work-related stuff too seriously. For me, it's just a job that provides me really good money to do what I really want to do."

As a police officer, Caitlin is more devoted to her job than Jessica is but equally determined to keep it separate from her personal life. "As much as I can, I try to relate to my work as though it's just a job, to maintain a sense of life outside of police work. I have friends who are not in law enforcement, who have interests that are different from mine and who keep me grounded." Staying connected to life outside the precinct house enables Caitlin to perform her professional duties without losing her civilian identity.

BASICALLY CLUELESS

When work becomes a source of connection, it gains in meaning. This begins with the relationships we make in our immediate work environment and radiates out to the larger world: the customers we serve, the impact of our work in the community, and the mysterious ways that what we do may be impacting the world outside our awareness.

Many times in my own life, the work I do has touched people in ways that I could not have predicted. For years, one of my heroes has been the Burmese political leader Aung San Suu Kyi. Although democratically elected to run the country in 1990, she was prevented by the military from taking office, having been placed under house arrest the previous year for her democratic activities. While detained she was awarded the 1991 Nobel Peace Prize.

Suu Kyi has said that there were times throughout her then six-year confinement when she was offered the opportunity to leave Burma, but it was clear that if she did she would not be allowed back in, thus abandoning the people who had chosen her as their leader. And so, even though she did not see her children or her husband for many years and was at times malnourished and ill, she chose to stay.

One of my primary meditation teachers, Sayadaw U Pandita is also from Burma. In 1984, he came to the United States for the first time to teach a three-month retreat at the Insight Meditation Society. Later some friends and I decided to make a book out of the talks he had given. I raised some money, found a transcriber, an editor, and a publisher, and the book *In This Very Life* came into being. I felt happy that I had done something to express gratitude to my teacher. As a classical and clear depiction of that particular lineage in the Buddhist meditative tradition, I knew it would help people, but also thought it possible that not all that many people would be drawn to such a classical approach. The book went into the minor good deed category in my mind.

In 1995, Suu Kyi was released from house arrest for a while, and she had an opportunity to speak to the outside world. In interviews and writings she said that during her years of house arrest, an important source of spiritual support had been U Pandita's book *In This Very Life*, which her husband had sent to her from England. Using the book, she had started to regularly meditate and, as she told one friend, that book had been her lifeline. Hearing that, I immediately took the book out of the "minor good deed" category, and put it in the "I wonder if this will be the best thing I will have done in my life" category. I had done something thinking it would have one kind of effect, and in a million years couldn't have predicted it would make its way back into Burma to support someone I considered a genuine hero.

That experience taught me to do the good that is right in front of me, even if it seems relatively small or inconsequential. I thought that someday I might write a book called *Basically Clueless,* because in so many ways we are. There is so much we just can't see or know right now, including precisely how our actions will ripple out. We help someone have a better day, and they may go out and encourage an employee or relax enough to see a creative option or forgive a minor transgression and give someone another chance.

Maria was privileged to feel the power of a small gesture, and never forgot it. As a young editor at a publishing house that was run by a tyrannical and moody publisher, Maria was often in the hot seat. With a new baby and a heavy workload, it wasn't too hard for her to feel frustrated to the point of tears. One day, after having been yelled at for the whole floor to hear, she left the building feeling horrible, wanting to quit, feeling that her child would look on her as a failure if she were to ever see the way Maria was treated. When she came back, there was a little box of candy on her office chair with a note: "Noticed you were having a hard day. Hope this helps." It was from a young assistant, whom Maria did not even know particularly well, who just wanted to offer solace. Maria was affected deeply by the generosity and pays it forward, in the name of her friend, whenever she can. The assistant's name was Michelle and while they've lost touch, Michelle's generosity is still a part of the world at large.

We cannot always know how our work contributions are affecting others. This is where trust comes in. When we work with a positive intention, even when our tasks seem somewhat trivial, our actions will have positive results. "Small things with great love," Mother Teresa counseled individuals worried that their work was meaningless. In other words, what we do is frequently less important than how we do it. I heard a wonderful story about a dramaturge—a person trained to work with playwrights—who believed that her work was unimportant in a world where people are starving. This woman, we'll call her Ann, dreamed of moving to Calcutta to help Mother Teresa in her mission to feed "the poorest of the poor." When Mother Teresa arrived in Ann's home city to receive a humanitarian award, Ann waited outside the hotel where Mother Teresa was staying, eager to offer her services. Finally, a car pulled up and out stepped the tiny reverend mother in her blue-and-white sari. Ann told Mother Teresa about her dream of giving up her work in the theater in order to come to India and do some real good. Mother Teresa listened patiently to her story then inquired into her line of work. When Ann told her that she helped people put on plays, the old nun smiled and took her hand. "No, dear!" she said. "You must stay here and work. Just do it with an open heart. In this country, there is a famine of the spirit. Stay here and feed *your* people."

Most of us want to believe that the work we do is connected to a cause greater than ourselves. We long to know that we are working and living for a bigger purpose. Yet herein

Stealth Meditation

Look for ways to acknowledge someone's challenges. Even when you can't fix things, people appreciate the recognition that the workload is growing, the new deadline is a killer, that it's hard to deal with others' grumpiness.

lies a paradox critical to wisdom and well-being. For our work to be of maximum benefit, we need to let it go. For our contribution to help the community, we need to remember that it's not about us. We work with an open heart and the best intentions and trust in life to do the rest. This is the essence of trust, which is not something that we possess but something that we *do*, a willingness to take the next step.

In the work we do, we remind ourselves that we cannot control how others will ultimately react to our efforts. We can only do our best to make a difference. We can maintain an awareness of how little we actually know about how our work will finally impact the world and do our best to remain connected to our own creativity and caring. When we approach work in a creative spirit (which is possible no matter our occupation), learning from daily experience, we remain engaged and enlivened.

When we remember that the work we do does matter, however inconsequential the task, and that our personal worth does not rise or fall with professional standing or reputation, we can then perform it with an open heart and be grateful to others. Gina LaRoche of Seven Stones Leadership writes, "Today I am profoundly grateful for all who serve me. I do not take for granted the newspaper delivery, the recycling pickup, the bus driver, the barista, the security guard, the cashier, the person who cooked my lunch, bagged my groceries, or hung my dry cleaning." Just as others serve us, we are able to serve others. By disentangling work from self-worth and remembering that we're good enough—already blessed by life and a capacity for wisdom and love—regardless of our salary or job description, we learn to approach our work with insight and generosity. We learn that creativity comes from within—how we see, what we notice, when we help, whom we touch—and is always available to us when we are paying attention. This choice to be awake at work can change the most seemingly meaningless employment into an opportunity for connection, creativity, and personal growth.

EXERCISE: Articulate Your Own Mission

How do you find your core intention? How can you discern your passion and purpose on the planet? One fun way to do this is by identifying one or two qualities that make up the very core of who you are. Having a personal mission is such an important part of so many dimensions of a liberated life—including one's livelihood.

Look at the list of verbs that follow. As you look at each word, say it aloud and allow a full minute to register how much each particular quality resonates with you. Then write a number next to the word, using a rating scale of 1 to 5. If you feel nothing at all about the word, give it a 1. If you're ready to jump out of your chair because you feel so in tune with that quality, give it a 5.

- Bridging
- Brightening
- Communicating
- Connecting
- Creating
- Discovering
- Embracing
- Encouraging
- Giving
- Healing

- Integrating
- Leading
- Learning
- Loving
- Organizing
- Relating
- Remembering
- Restoring
- Teaching

And you may find there are some powerful verbs not included on this list that you want to add. Go for it!

Now look at your numbers—every word that you've rated with a 4 or 5 should make it into your mission statement. My key words are "discovering" and "connecting." These words describe both what makes me feel most alive as well as how I am here to serve others. I am at my best when I embody discovery and connection and when I am helping other people to discover and connect.

Your words can become the beginning of clarifying your personal mission. Once you've come up with a list, consider how much your current work situation allows you to experience these qualities.

When you come to the end of this exercise, consider if and in what ways you can bring a new sensibility to work to even more align your livelihood with these deeper ambitions and longings.

~~~~~~

EXERCISE: **Moving from the What to the How**

Think of a specific task at work—teaching a child to read, preserving a client's wealth, protecting the rights of an elderly nursing home resident—whatever it might be. As you establish a metric for success, add a dimension of how you are doing the work. How focused are you at meetings? How much patience and compassion are you bringing forth? When you've been impatient or distracted, how gracefully have you been able to begin again? Rather than viewing those elements as superfluous, recognize that they are a large measure of finding fulfillment and meaning at work. They also may have a ripple effect of positivity that you may never know, but that improves lives nonetheless.

EXERCISE: Basically Clueless, Planting Seeds

Write down something you would very much like to accomplish at work—a new project, an innovation, a big departure from the current routine. In one column, write down everything over which you have direct control—your own attitude and input, of course, but also whatever policies or procedures you can mold on your own. In another column, write down whomever or whatever would have a role in determining this outcome—your boss, your clients, economic trends—whatever comes to mind. When you're done, look at the lists.

So many times, we take to heart and feel responsible for too many things on that second list. I have friends who were inconsolable about losing jobs. In addition to economic pressures and hardships from the loss, they seemed to blame themselves for everything—the worldwide economic collapse, the retooling of their industry. With that feeling, it's especially hard to start over.

The healing effect of this exercise is similar to the serenity prayer: Grant me the serenity to accept the things I cannot change, the courage to change the things I can, and the wisdom to know the difference.

Seeing those two lists empowers us. They are a good reminder of the interconnected world we live in. That first list reminds us of the importance of our planting seeds—we have to do our part or nothing will happen. The second reminds us to acknowledge other forces and to be open as we try to make a difference.

Q & A

Q When I look back at what used to drive me to success, it was really ego. Now that I've discovered the benefits of meditation, I think of my life simply in terms of how I want to live with mindfulness. How do I reconcile that with my work?

A Your work can fit into the larger vision of what is important in your life instead of defining all that is and will remain significant. We can have an impact on the world doing all kinds of work. When we feel driven to succeed, it can be very energizing, but we might also question what is compromised or sacrificed for success. What we find energizing at one point in our lives might prove exhausting at another—we can be so hell-bent on success that we drive ourselves into loneliness and alienation. Reflecting on how to find your own deeper happiness, perhaps outside of your work, isn't a selfish or superficial thing. It is the fuel for sustaining effort at work without damage to yourself and those you care about.

Q I tend to focus on meditating when I'm feeling stressed at work but often forget about it when things are going well.

A Meditation can have a beneficial effect whatever we're encountering at work. It helps us appreciate easy and joyous times more by reminding us to recognize and focus on them. It helps in times of stress to give us greater resiliency so that we are not so overwhelmed by the difficulty. And it helps in ordinary, repetitious, routine times, too, so that we have a more acute sense of awareness and connection than we otherwise might. Sometimes the easiest way to establish a regular practice is to create a realistic and achievable commitment, such as meditating every day—even just five minutes—for the next month or so. After the month, we can decide whether to renew or change the commitment.

CHAPTER 8

Open Awareness

OPEN AWARENESS REFERS TO OUR ABILITY to observe conditions as they are without feeling the need to change them. While this may sound passive to our action-oriented ears, the ability to rest comfortably in the present moment regardless of its imperfections is the foundation of all true happiness. Open awareness leads to acceptance. Acceptance leads to the end of conflict. The cessation of conflict leads to clarity of purpose and vision, which leads, in turn, to skillful action. Open awareness leaves nothing out, including our basic cluelessness about what our work will mean in the long run. This allows us to relax, to expand rather than contract, to take the long view, and to stay open to all possibilities. At work, this awareness helps us give colleagues the benefit of the doubt; endows us with patience to deal with the inevitable slings and arrows of employment; provides a more amenable attitude toward suggestions, criticism, disappointment; enables us to do our jobs with more generous and collegial spirits; and instills in us the capacity to keep an open mind and view our work, no matter how modest, as service in the larger world.

THE ANGLE OF VISION

"What is life, but the angle of vision?" Ralph Waldo Emerson asked. This profound truth applies as much to work as it does to all our activities. Life is *how* we see it. The world is how we engage it. Work is how we do it. We create our suffering or promote our happiness depending on the clarity of our perspective, the approach we choose, and our ability to see interconnection. Understanding ourselves as parts of a greater whole is the key to open awareness, the eighth pillar of happiness at work.

If there is one emotional refrain that I hear again and again, it is that people feel their jobs limit rather than expand their lives and make their existence less powerful than it would be if they won the lottery. This sense of diminishment, of shrinking to fit the necessities of earning a living, often filters into feelings of bitterness that find their way into the workplace.

John, a magazine editor, experienced a dramatic opening of awareness toward his job when the company he worked for—a corporation known for its stingy, worker-unfriendly policies—displayed unexpected generosity to John when his wife was diagnosed with cancer. In the five years he'd worked there, John was chronically unhappy over the organization's chilly treatment of its employees. Working for an officious boss (the kind who questions each expense account receipt), John had been white-knuckling it in a company whose ethos he deplored and a job he dreamed of leaving.

When John's wife got sick, he expected his boss to be unsympathetic, but quite the opposite turned out to be true. This typically starchy, difficult woman was exceptionally kind toward John when he told her the news, and granted him a two-month paid leave of absence with no questions asked. John's colleagues, who were usually so self-absorbed that they barely spoke to one another, called him on speakerphone every couple of weeks to keep him abreast of changes at the office, and to find out how he was holding up.

When John finally returned to work, he was startled to realize that his angle of vision had changed dramatically. "I saw that I'd been making a difficult situation intolerable," he now understands, "seeing everything through a negative lens, expecting the worst and getting it." This was the same boss, and the same colleagues, but after they opened their hearts to him, John's heart opened, too. "It was surreal, almost like having a veil removed. Not that my boss turned into an angel. She's still demanding and often annoying, but once I could see another dimension of her personality, everything changed, including the quality of my work. I was assigned two cover stories in the six months after my leave of absence. That had never happened before. The change came because I had opened up. It taught me that we really do paint the world with our own eyes. I knew this before, but only intellectually. This experience woke me up." When we understand the importance of our angle of vision, we can transform our quality of awareness. This can provide a refuge of peace regardless of the circumstances.

As Elizabeth, a conference manager, describes: "Recently, there was a morning when I felt anxious going into work. I had a 9:00 a.m. meeting, a 9:30 meeting, a 10:00 a.m. meeting, and a 12:30 lunch. I also had to put together a PowerPoint presentation by the end of the day. I am not very good in PowerPoint—prone to panicking and calling the IT department and saying things like, 'I pressed a button, and all the slides on the left disappeared.'

"It wasn't until I was walking across the parking lot in the evening that I had any time to reflect on the day, but as I did, I was kind of laughing as I remembered things that had happened, and thinking how everybody had been so nice! I cannot convey what a rare thought that is. In fact, in the five years I have been with the company, that might have been the first time I had thought about it in such an all-encompassing way. Of course, it's an office of human beings, so there is always going to be the possibility of bad behavior—including my own! But as I walked to my car, I realized that although I didn't have a perfect day—I complained too much about an email I'd received, I checked Facebook multiple times, and I ignored some other work to get the presentation done—I was happy. Even more interesting, I was aware of being happy and of not shutting it down with follow-up thoughts about why I shouldn't be happy."

Awareness is malleable and never fixed. Moment to moment, we choose the view and attitude that color our reality. Sometimes what's required are concentration and one-pointed attention. Other times we use open awareness to widen our lens and take in the big picture. When we do this at work, we release attachment to personal agendas—the need to be special, the thirst for praise, the stranglehold of competition, the fear of losing our turf—and see ourselves as parts of something larger. Self-centeredness is exchanged for camaraderie; control is exchanged for surrender; personal ambition is tempered by empathy and deeply caring about the people around us.

Stealth Meditation

If you find yourself straining to think "outside the box," explore what made up that box. Understanding how you got to where you are is the first step in going beyond that point.

But what about ambition? What about achievement and healthy competition? Many of us fear that we'll lose our edge if we become too generous and open. Being happy at work requires that we question this assumption. In the dog-eat-dog paradigm, where everyone is out for him- or herself, there is never enough for everyone and your win is my loss. According to this narrow view, we must keep the focus on personal achievement in order not to be eclipsed. But this scarcity model is obsolete, uninspiring, and terribly lonely. It can lead to what's called "the achievement trap," where our angle of vision is obsessively focused on getting ahead regardless of the cost.

LEADERSHIP

A wider view describes how organizations themselves can change as they open up, and their organizational culture becomes more imbued with mindfulness and compassion.

Yet a more narrow view often trickles down from the top. Instructing leaders in how to help create a greater culture of openness in the workplace, Michael Carroll counsels some of his very successful clients to consider how they *see*, shifting the focus from pure profit motive to sensitivity toward the people who work for them.

"I tell them that they wouldn't be where they are in their careers if they weren't good at getting stuff done. But for them to develop as truly distinctive leaders, we will need to focus less on what they do for a living and focus more on what they see for a living." Whether or not we seek leadership roles at work, this "seeing"—by which Carroll means open awareness—is a key ingredient to happiness at work. When we move from being self-focused to being mindful of the whole picture, we grow as individuals, do a better job, deepen our relationships to colleagues, and remain open to change and flexible in our expectations. Without learning to "see" wisely, even the most talented may fail to connect with others or reach their full creative potential. According to Carroll, it is from how well leaders see the workplace that they're able to respond mindfully and sensitively to their employees. The reverse is equally true: When employees use open awareness at work, their ability to cooperate and maximize their skills improves proportionately. Many bosses are trained to be more concerned with the bottom line than with the workplace as a whole, just as many of the people who work for them see their job as a paycheck, and shrink their perspective accordingly. Reorienting leaders and employees from the "doing" model to the "seeing" one, Carroll is able to help them open their awareness. "What they require is a form of wisdom beyond doing, accomplishing, and achieving," he says. Instead, mindful leaders and employees can begin to make their goal "to discern, recognize, and understand."

Take the case of Susan, a corporate CEO fired unexpectedly from her job as the head of a multinational entertainment company. Susan had been a master of "doing." For three decades, she'd been clawing her way to the top of the corporate hierarchy, focused exclusively on her own success while ignoring the needs of her employees. Known as a brilliant, if maniacal, leader, she'd spent her career obsessed with profits, reputation, and protecting her position at the head of the conference table. Respected and despised in equal measure, she was one of those "sacred monsters" who populate the upper echelons of cutthroat businesses and appear invincible to the people who work for them.

Suddenly fired, Susan found herself jobless for the first time in decades and was forced to take a good hard look at who she had become. Unhappy with what she saw—"I was a witch," she admits—Susan began a soul-searching process that led her to the meditation cushion. "I needed to drop the masks, get real, face the ways in which I'd hurt people—and begin to forgive myself—before I could look for another job." She found this "dark night of the soul" to be grueling. In addition to mindfulness practice, Susan began to see a therapist, who helped her with the deconstruction of a persona she could no longer live with. "I saw how much I hated myself," she says with some surprise. "I saw how much I didn't *see*. I realized how I'd used work as a suit of armor to protect myself from being attacked by others. My therapist helped me see that I'd been protecting myself this way since childhood," she says. "I'd been hiding my whole life behind this mask of authority. Not until it was taken away from me did I realize how trapped I was."

After two years of introspective practice, Susan returned to the entertainment business with a radically different outlook. "I realized I wasn't invincible and that gave me more compassion. I saw how quickly it all can change—one phone call and my world crashed down—and this made me take myself much less seriously." In her current job as the president of another major entertainment company, Susan is determined to do things differently. "It's a struggle," she admits. "Old habits die hard. I can still be a major bitch under pressure, but now I can *see* what I'm doing and am not so resistant to making amends. When I backslide these days, at least I can admit it. It's no longer me against the world. I recognize that I'm vulnerable, and also responsible to the people who work for me. Before, I didn't understand this. I was arrogant and that's why I needed this lesson."

Surrender can be a sign of strength, for bosses as well as employees. Although we rarely think of leadership and surrender as complementary (since society labels surrender a form of weakness), surrender can be among the greatest of leadership skills. Surrender signals open awareness regardless of where we find ourselves in the pecking order, not giving up or giving in, but learning to let go of the need for self-centered control. This echoes an old adage in Zen Buddhism, where it is said that the aspiration of good teachers is to have students who surpass them in wisdom and compassion. The teacher exists to serve the students, helping them excel, rather than basking in the glory of their ego being stroked by admiration.

> **Stealth Meditation**
> Travel to work some days without a radio, iPod, book, or phone. Experience the transition from home to work as a journey unto itself.

Thus viewed, the purpose of leadership in any domain is not to shine the spotlight on oneself, but on others. Then each of those affected might themselves affect countless more. Realizing this, employers help to create an environment where workers feel valued rather than dominated, encouraged rather than held back. Surrender allows a leader to get out of his or her own way and focus instead on unlocking the potential of those whom they serve—the employees who need leadership to thrive.

Using mindfulness to open our awareness, stepping beyond self-centered focus, we come to see that for bosses and employees alike, the achievement compulsion driving our society—while not necessarily harmful in itself—can easily blind us to interconnection and preclude peace.

OPENNESS

Open awareness, the capacity to see the big picture with acceptance, provides us with a stronger foundation at work and helps us remain upright in the face of stress, uncertainty, and conflict. Cultivating this at work creates strength and balance, as well as a heightened sense of well-being. In this happier state, we're able to be aware of whatever is happening without our mind or heart resisting or contracting. We find it easier to separate people from their actions and to agree and disagree without creating enmity or conflict. A self-employed interior designer named Rachel discovered this for herself. Before she started meditating, Rachel's work life was filled with fear. As a freelancer in a sinking economy, she devoted as much energy to "staving off the barbarian hordes,"—meaning her competitors—as she did to being creative and satisfying her customers. "No matter how well I was doing, it never seemed to be enough. I felt like a guppy in a shark tank. I knew I was good and my customers loved me but that didn't make any difference. Inside I was a wobbly mess." Rachel's awareness was trained on failure and closed to the fact that she was successful. From this narrow vantage point, she saw only danger, smallness, and looming destruction of a beloved business she'd built from scratch.

To counter her anxiety, Rachel sought help from a meditation teacher who held weekly sessions at her local temple. After learning to follow her breath—"sheer hell," as Rachel describes it—she discovered after a month or so that the "balled-up fist" in her solar plexus was starting to open. "When I could manage to shift my attention away from obsessive worrying, even for a few minutes, I started to open. I wasn't doing anything to make it happen. I just started to loosen up, little by little. I felt increasingly less tormented. The calmer I felt, the stronger I felt. Once I learned how to shift my attention away from the doomsday scenario I carried around with me in my head, other information could get in. Beginning with the fact that I'm a very good designer and my customers, at least so far, have remained loyal to me. Also, if things do go wrong and I go out of business, God forbid, I will survive. I could never have said that before without getting depressed. Now I know that I'm bigger than the fear. My feet are more on the ground. I no longer pretend that I can control the future."

That's how open awareness works: In the space created by mindfulness, we remember our true identity, which isn't defined by our circumstances—the ups and downs of everyday life—but is capable of being powerful, clear, and free.

Rob, a musical conductor, was attending his first retreat at the Insight Meditation Society (IMS). We knew he'd have to interrupt his retreat briefly and go back to New York to conduct a tribute concert at Carnegie Hall. We planned his sojourn into the city carefully to help preserve the intensity of the retreat. Rob decided not to go home for the night, but to stay at a hotel where he wouldn't be confronted by mail, messages, and obligations, and could just be quiet.

At IMS everyone is asked to do a chore for the duration of their stay. Rob's was helping to keep a particular bathroom clean. Upon his return, he told me a very funny story. He was standing on the beautiful stage at Carnegie Hall, conducting the orchestra, on a majestic occasion, and his mind flashed back to that bathroom, thinking, "I hope someone is helping keep it clean while I'm gone." Who was he in that moment, the lauded conductor or the meditator with a humble chore? Actually, because he could shift between both, he was defined by neither, and he was limitless.

Rob goes on to describe his experience: "I was speaking to a full house at Carnegie with ease, not only totally calm but feeling so connected to the audience that it felt only like sharing, not like me and them, but us all together, all one soul. It was the same with the orchestra. And after the concert, one of the musicians told me how much they appreciated how I'd allowed them to play fully and directly, without interference from my ego. I had the feeling that day that I am just a chimney gathering up all the energy from the musicians (souls) surrounding me and sending the combined energies upward. And then feeling it spread over the audience who send it through themselves to the orchestra and back through me into an energy soul cycle."

GETTING OUT OF THE WAY

We need not invent a false sense of strength to buttress our illusions. We need only to quiet our minds enough to remember the potential that lies underneath the circumstance we find ourselves in. When I was working on an earlier book *Faith,* I had several points of writer's block and significant struggle. At one point I was talking to Susan Griffin, a wonderful writer and writing coach, about my woes. She listened for a long time, then advised, "You have to stop thinking of yourself as the person writing this book, and see yourself as the first person who gets to read this book."

She was totally right. Seeing myself as "the author" led to terrible ego striving—I was afraid of not doing the subject justice, so I got too abstract and philosophical. I was afraid of being too simple, so my writing got more elaborate and unnatural and felt phony. I was afraid of my choice of topic (several people had warned me against it) and kept second-guessing myself. When instead, I thought of myself as the first person who gets to see the work, I was so happy. I stepped out of the way, let the writing flow through me, and felt blessed. I felt like I'd created something that I could use and be proud of.

Susan also said to me, "A lot of people might assume you write a book about a topic like that because you know all about it, and you want to impart your expertise. More likely you are writing a book about a topic like that because you feel a need to explore it, and the writing is part of the exploration." Here, too, she was completely correct. When I was frozen into the role of the "expert," my writing froze, too, in a highfalutin, unpleasant way. When I was open to the force of exploration and discovery, wonder would often ensue. Open awareness enables us to relax even when work gets stressful, to make clearer choices, communicate more effectively, tell the truth, and be both more trusting and trustworthy.

Wise balance and a sense of proportion strengthen the foundation of open awareness. Untangling ourselves from rigid job identities enables us to do a better job. In turn, this sensitizes us to the world, making us aware of how our own actions and feelings affect people around us.

POSSIBILITIES

Open awareness makes us aware of creative options, ways in which our ordinary routines can be tweaked to become suddenly adventurous or joyous. Here's a story of men having fun on their job while doing good: Three men in Tennessee, while working for a commercial window cleaning business, American National Skyline, took on the challenge of bringing smiles to the young patients at Le Bonheur Children's Hospital in Memphis. Photos show the men using the same equipment they use to dangle in the air washing windows every working day, but this time dressed in Spider-Man costumes.

The men spent four hours visiting windows and spraying Silly String at the kids, who, for a brief while, were able to forget about their conditions and their fears and their pain and just enjoy themselves. One of the men, Steve Oszaniec, said, "We just went there, put on the costumes, and went up. The hospital staff brought a lot of the kids to the little family room there so they could see us. It was unbelievable. They just totally forgot they were sick for a minute. They were just ecstatic about it."

And open awareness makes us more aware of what we're good at, and sometimes wholly different ways to utilize our skills. I recently met an attorney whose specialty had been in trusts and estates. Even though she had a successful law career, she recognized that she wasn't very happy. She pondered her options and realized that she had very much enjoyed the informal fund-raising she had done for a friend's independent film. Through the open awareness she developed in her meditation practice, she was able to redefine her career, combining her skills and her enthusiasm to fund-raise for a large national nonprofit organization, specializing in planned giving, helping people draft trusts and estates for their philanthropic donations. In a similar way, my website designer friend, Marco, is exploring the world of fashion design. Because of the ability to see things in a new way, my accountant neighbor, Nadya, is looking for volunteer opportunities to teach financial literacy as the first step of discovering a new path.

In that space of openness, we can ask ourselves: What do I love to do? Could I use my skills in a way that is different from the way I'm using them now? Is there a new start stirring in my heart or an idea pressing to take form?

Even in bleak or traumatic circumstances, open awareness allows us to ask, can an endeavor, a possibility, a challenge be seen in a whole new way? In fact, many psychologists define trauma as a frozen state and depict healing as moving beyond our pattern of adhering to devastation. This can be true for communities as well. The 2011 documentary *The Interrupters* describes just such reenvisioning. It describes the Cease Fire initiative of the Chicago Project of Violence Prevention. An epidemiologist, Dr. Gary Slutkin, launched the project. His outside-the-box idea was describing violence as a public health issue that could be addressed the way an outbreak in an epidemic is addressed—go after the most infected and stop the infection at its source, taking lessons from the AIDS and tuberculosis epidemics he had witnessed in Africa. Tio Hardiman created the Violence Interruptors program within Cease Fire and now runs it. The Interruptors—men and women who have been gang members, who have been in prison and have returned to their neighborhoods—are committed to helping people find alternatives to the hopelessness all around them by interrupting cycles of violence they sense are about to erupt. On the streets, they hear whispers of revenge about to be sought, and they talk to the hurt and angry young man or woman. They build relationships with young people who feel they have nothing to look forward to. They mediate conflicts before they can explode. They listen deeply. From the first linking of violence to epidemics, through the program's bold and creative implementation, you can see the living example of Albert Einstein's adage, "We can't solve problems by using the same kind of thinking we used when we created them."

Stealth Meditation

If you are nervous about speaking before a group, spend a few moments doing a loving-kindness meditation before you get up to speak. This can allay feelings you may have of feeling judged or measured by the group. They are no different from you.

I believe we all have a touch of that genius within. And I believe we can all access that genius. I think of the words of Dr. Mae Jemison, "Don't let anyone rob you of your imagination, your creativity, or your curiosity. It's your place in the world; it's your life. Go on and do all you can with it, and make it the life you want to live."

We all can clear away the obstructions to our true potential, and to whole new ways of thinking. Suzanne Seggerman realized that through an unusual video game she received twenty years ago from a colleague. The game, Hidden Agenda, was a simple but compelling strategy game where the player is in the role of president of an imaginary Central American country. It surprised her by deeply affecting her understanding of the real world current events she was reading about. By putting her in the driver's seat—giving her the power to make the decisions affecting her virtual country and its people—she was able to see the issues in a deeper light. By experiencing the decision-making process firsthand, she understood the complexities of that process as never before.

It was a cathartic moment for Suzanne—and she came to view video games as a platform for much more than just entertainment; she realized that they might even have the power to change the world. It was a novel concept, but one that she embraced after a simple shifting of her viewpoint to a new way of thinking.

In the summer of 2004, Suzanne launched Games for Change at an exploratory conference with other non-profit innovators. Its mission is to facilitate the creation and distribution of social impact games that can serve in humanitarian and educational efforts. In just a few years, the company was partnering with major media companies MTV and Microsoft. The MacArthur Foundation was supporting a new research lab she had cofounded at the New School in New York City to test and evaluate these new kinds of games.

Suzanne says, "I came to meditation a few years after the launch of Games for Change, and it made an enormous difference in my work life. I had never run a nonprofit before, and I had lots of fears about taking on such a big responsibility. There was a steady dialogue of doubts in my mind: You have no leadership ability; you can't possibly run this thing; you're a total fake. Once I started to meditate, I came to see these as thoughts, not truths. There might have been some truth in them—I did have a lot to learn—but meditation helped me better sort through them. I was able to have more compassion toward my weaknesses and also have more faith in my strengths. It also helped me to redirect my energies: Instead of lingering on my doubts, I was able to instead focus on my own passion and beliefs—that which I knew to be true—that games had an extraordinary power for good that people were failing to see. Once I kept my eye on the reality, I let myself be driven by the facts and not the fears."

This is what happens when we open our imaginations. People tend to think of mindfulness as a sober, even dull activity, but the opposite is true. Mindfulness reveals our options to us. It reminds us where the deepest happiness can be found.

Bill Ford, Ford Motor Company executive chairman, credits his meditation practice with helping him steer his company through the massive disruption and contraction of a terrible recession. He says, "During the darkest era, when it really felt like we might lose absolutely everything, I'd lay in bed thinking, *What would it be like to lose everything? What would it be like to lose absolutely everything, including a large part of my own identity?* But I realized through practice that it wasn't my identity—that the core of *me* would be just fine. That the people I loved and cared about would still love and care about me. And that sounds fairly trite, but I also know that had I not been practicing for a little bit of time, I think I would have understood that intellectually, but I wouldn't have understood it in my heart. To me that was the best grounding that I could have had during an extremely difficult period, because losing everything really didn't mean losing everything."

In looking ahead, Bill Ford sees a very different, integrated future for transportation, where instead of a person or family owning their own car, each individual trip might be custom designed just for you, with a car or bicycle you pick up and leave and buses and trains all figuring into a new and personalized way of getting from here to there. For the scion of a car company, this really is a new way of thinking: "I believe we're going to have to have every form of transportation—cars, bicycles, buses, taxis, subways, pedestrians—all in a single network, all talking to one another, and all optimizing the ability to move around."

Thomas Edison once said, "I have not failed. I've just found 10,000 ways that won't work." Edison is famous not only for his inventions, but also for his views on work—the resoluteness, the energy (he called it "perspiration"), and the sheer ability to keep going even in the face of seeming defeat. This is echoed in advice on creativity from Stanford Technology Ventures director Tina Seelig: "Scientists have another name for failure: data." And advice on writing from film critic Roger Ebert: "Start. Don't look back. If at the end it doesn't meet your hopes, start again. Now you know more about your hopes."

Stealth Meditation

Think about whose work makes your job possible—housekeeper, technician, bookkeeper, elevator operator, fund-raiser—and thank them.

Fostering greater balance of heart and mind is a key to uncovering our immense capacity for creativity, and a valuable avenue to cultivating this balance is meditation practice. Meditation helps us see our own difficult mind states—such as anger or fear or bitterness or an awful sense of helplessness—with compassion rather than self-judgment.

Meditation provides a refuge during life's tumultuous storms by helping us connect compassionately with ourselves and with others, no matter the circumstances, so that difficulty doesn't lead to alienation. Meditation also helps us awaken to joy and animates our ordinary routine so that it comes alive for us. The spaciousness of mind and greater ease of heart that naturally arise through concentration, mindfulness, and compassion are fundamental components of an open and renewed spirit.

Being happy at work is possible for all of us, anytime and anywhere, with open eyes and a caring heart. We need only to take the first step.

MEDITATION: Open Awareness

Sit comfortably or lie down. Allow your gentle focus to come to what you are hearing. Notice that even as we like certain sounds and we don't like others, we don't have to chase after them, to hold on to or push them away, fretfully trying to seize control over that which we will never have control over. Some lovely sounds arise, others are quite unpleasant or jangly. Practice simply being present as hearing arises. Notice the sound for what it is; you don't have to elaborate. If you find yourself thinking, *Oh, that's a bus. I wonder what the bus route is? Maybe they should change the bus route, so it's more convenient for me,* see if you can gently let go of your thoughts and simply hear.

Hear the sounds that arise and pass away as though they're washing through you. There's nothing you need to do about them. You don't need to respond to them; you needn't try to stop them; you don't even have to understand them.

Let your mind become like a big empty sky, an empty space. Different sounds are appearing and changing and vanishing in the open space of the mind. You're not looking for sounds, but rather simply opening up to them. You don't have to send your ears out to listen.

Feel the space within which you're sitting. Feel the ground underneath you, supporting you. Notice yourself in the space. You don't need to reach out; you can trust the space to support you so that you can relax. Notice how the earth is supporting you. You don't have to manufacture that or be responsible for it. Just receive it and trust it.

Open to the different sensations in your body that arise and disappear as points of feeling, like stars in the night sky. There's no inside, no outside, no boundaries of separation, only sounds, sensations, appearing and disappearing in the open space of mind. Notice how effortlessly each sound is known in the moment it appears. Notice how effortlessly each sensation is known in the moment it appears.

Be aware of thoughts and images, like clouds in the sky, just appearing and disappearing, in the open, empty space of mind. There's no inside, no outside, no boundaries of separation, just sounds, sensations, thoughts, and images, appearing and dissolving in the open emptiness of mind. Not wanting, not looking, simply resting, in the empty, aware space of mind.

As sounds appear, sensations appear, as points of feeling, thoughts, and images appear, simply rest. No wanting, no doing, all experience appears and changes and disappears by itself as you experience the vastness of consciousness itself.

And when you feel ready, you can end the meditation and see what it is like to bring this sense of open awareness to your day.

～～～～～

EXERCISE: Opening and Closing

In this exercise, we'll look at the process of self-contraction: the times when we identify with a particular phenomenon, or get lost in clinging or condemning, and lose the perspective of open awareness.

Throughout the day, look for the moments when you find yourself either hating what you are feeling or convinced it will last forever. Explore what happens in your body, in your mood, as you relax and connect to the same emotion with more spaciousness. Describe your experience of relating to the same feeling in different ways—condemning yourself for feeling it, thinking it is all you will ever feel, or returning to a "big mind" perspective even if the emotion itself remains. Particularly look for moments of:

- Anger
- Desire
- Judgment
- Self-judgment

- Restlessness
- Delight
- Uncertainty

~~~~~~

EXERCISE: When Things Go Wrong

In India, they use a parable about a kind of monkey trap in which sticky tar is spread on the ground. When the monkey comes along, it steps in the tar with one foot and gets stuck. In trying to extricate itself, the monkey puts down its other foot, then a hand, then another hand, and then its head. Finally, it is one stuck monkey.

This parable is a description of how we can either limit our efforts for freedom to the same sticky patch, not utilizing creative thinking or different approaches, or we can take a new look at what's around us, and reach out to grab a nearby tree or the helping hands of others, to hoist ourselves free. That's the opportunity we have: to recognize that we're getting stuck, trapped in old habits, and take the chance to make a big shift and not keep going in the same old way.

As either a reflection or a writing exercise, the next time you feel stuck, picture that poor monkey once stuck and now free and imagine how he might have gotten free. Have fun with any scenario you can imagine.

Then consider how you might currently be stuck in your work or your life. Take a big, expansive, panoramic view. How might that change?

~~~~~~~~

EXERCISE: Starting Again

In many ways, the journey to real happiness at work rests all along on the first skill we practiced—the ability to continually begin again. We started the meditations contained in this book with a practice of resting our attention on the feeling of the breath and, very importantly, being able to return our attention there once distracted, without spinning off into harsh self-judgment or soliloquies of despair. With a full heart and kindness toward ourselves, we need to continually be able to begin again. This is what creativity is, and what resilience is. We steer off course or make a mistake or lose sight of our aspiration, and amazingly, we can adjust and start over.

Reflect on a past experience at work and what happened as you faced an obstacle. Did you feel defeated and give up? If so, looking back, do you think that that was a good assessment or a loss of perspective?

If you now think there were options you couldn't see, primarily because of demoralization, envision how a committed practice of beginning again might change things.

I have a friend who, after an injury to his hands, has been told by his occupational therapist that as he moves to full use of his hands again, he needs to visualize an act just prior to doing it— reaching to pick up a cup, for example, or with a fork to pick up a piece of food. The visualization sets the stage for the mind to redefine what is possible.

In that spirit, envision something you'd like to see happen at work in the future. With that imagery, commit to bringing greater mindfulness, concentration, and loving-kindness to work, supported by the wonderful, renewing power of being able to begin again.

Q & A

Can I really be an effective leader and be kind at the same time?

Yes. People bring so many aspects of their lives into work, acknowledged or unacknowledged—a sick child, a friend's triumph, an overdue bill, a longed-for change. Kindness helps us see people for the intricate beings that we are, and leadership skills help us foster people's strengths so that they themselves can shine. Remember kindness doesn't mean weakness or not having standards. Kindness and discernment work together. There was a manager I knew who would hire people he just knew were good at something, even if *what* they were good at wasn't immediately apparent. Through patience and discernment, he would see their strengths, and their jobs would become clear. This was not a manager you'd consider warm and fuzzy. He was kind and smart and very successful at hiring the right people to staff a long-lasting and high-income producing company in a very competitive field.

Q What's your thirty-second pitch that I can use to help others understand how meditation would help a person be on top of their game at work?

A Much of our day we are pushed around by unhelpful habits such as being distracted or disconnected, holding on too long when circumstances have already changed, or not being wholehearted in pursuing an opportunity. Meditation can open us to alternative responses such as focus, awareness, and productive questioning and that leads to more fulfillment and better work.

Q How do I foster a team spirit behind these values if not everyone wants to take up meditation?

A Certainly not everyone wants to take up meditation, but most people can feel an alignment with values like mutual respect, insightful investigation, listening to one another. Meditation is a way to help those values become real in day-to-day life, helping people to understand themselves more and more and have a way to not get lost in old patterns. But it is best seen as a means to an end and not the end itself.

SOURCES

～～～

INTRODUCTION

Michael Carroll, *Awake at Work* (Boston: Shambhala, 2004)

CHAPTER 1: Balance

Bonnie J. Horrigan and Richard Davidson, "Meditation and Neuroplasticity: Training Your Brain," *Explore* 1, No. 5 (2005).

Quoted in David Gelles, "The Mind Business," *Financial Times* magazine, August 24, 2012, ft.com.

Quoted in Jen Weigel, "Be More Mindful for a Better Workplace," *Chicago Tribune,* August 21, 2012, articles.chicagotribune.com.

Daniel Goleman, *Emotional Intelligence: Why It Can Matter More Than IQ* (Bantam Books, 2005).

Melissa Kirsch, "Meditation at Work: Breathing Lessons," *Huffington Post,* March 9, 2011, huffingtonpost.com/melissa-kirsch/meditation-at-work_b_831838.html.

Casey Sheahan, Interview with the author, October 2012.

Quoted in Mark Matousek, "The Breath of Freedom," *Psychology Today,* December 10, 2012, psychologytoday.com.

"Volunteering Our Time Makes Us Feel Like We Have More Time: Study," *Huffington Post,* July 22, 2012, huffingtonpost.com/2012/07/22/volunteering-time_n_1672170.html.

"Giving Time Can Give You Time," *Association for Psychological Science* press release, July 12, 2012, psychologicalscience.org.

Gardiner Morse, "The Science Behind the Smile," *Harvard Business Review,* January–February 2012, hbr.org/2012/01/the-science-behind-the-smile/ar/1.

"How to Set Boundaries at Work," *Must Life,* 2012, mustlife.com/career-1/career-1-4420.html.

CHAPTER 2: Concentration

Quoted in Jen Weigel, "Be More Mindful for a Better Workplace," *Chicago Tribune*, August 21, 2012, articles.chicagotribune.com.

Alorie Gilbert, "Newsmaker: Why Can't You Pay Attention Anymore?" *CNET*, March 25, 2005, news.cnet.com/2100-1022_3-5637632.html.

Peter Toohey, *Boredom: A Lively History* (Yale University Press, 2011).

Arnie Kozak, "Boredom and Mindfulness," *Mindfulness Matters*, June 22, 2011, blog.beliefnet.com/mindfulness-matters/2011/06/boredom-and-mindfulness.html.

Joseph Ferrari and Timothy Pychyl, *Procrastination: Current Issues and New Directions* (Select Press, 2000).

CHAPTER 3: Compassion

Mark Matousek, *Ethical Wisdom, The Search for a Moral Life* (Anchor Books, 2012): page 75.

Jen Weigel, "Be More Mindful for a Better Workplace," *Chicago Tribune*, August 21, 2012, articles.chicagotribune.com.

Kristin Neff, *Self-Compassion: Stop Beating Yourself Up and Leave Insecurity Behind* (William Morrow, 2011).

CHAPTER 4: Resilience

Tony Schwartz, "Relax! You'll Be More Productive," *The New York Times*, February 9, 2013, nytimes.com.

Quoted in Jen Weigel, "Be More Mindful for a Better Workplace," *Chicago Tribune*, August 21, 2012, articles.chicagotribune.com.

Charles Tilly, "The Tyranny of the Here and Now," *Sociological Forum* (Springer, 1986): page 179.

Casey Sheahan, Interview with the author, October 2012.

Olivia Solon, "Compassion Over Empathy Could Help Prevent Emotional Burnout," *Wired.co.uk*, July 12, 2012, wired.co.uk.

Elie Calhoun, "Three Things That Separate the Good Aid Workers from the Burn-Outs," *Expat Backup* magazine, May 20, 2011, expatbackup.com/.

Maia Szalavitz, "How Your Brain Tells You When It's Time for a Break,"

TIME.com, January 31, 2013, healthland.time.com.

Marianne Elliott, *Zen Under Fire* (Sourcebooks, 2013).

CHAPTER 5: Communication and Connection

Cheri Maples quote, from conversation with author

Will Coldwell, "Mental Health Academic Warns of Reality TV 'Threat to British Psyche,'" *The Independent,* November 12, 2012, independent .co.uk.

Albert Mehrabian, *Silent Messages: Implicit Communication of Emotions and Attitudes* (Wadsworth Publishing Company, 1972).

Susan Cain, "The Rise of the New Groupthink," *The New York Times,* January 13, 2012, nytimes.com.

Exercise adapted from Leslie Booker's work at the Urban Sangha Project.

Exercise adapted from *Appreciative Inquiry Handbook,* by Cooperrider, Whitney, and Stavros.

CHAPTER 6: Integrity

Joan Duncan Oliver, "She's Got the Beat," *Tricycle* magazine, Winter 2009, tricycle.com/how-we-live/shes-got-beat?page=0,0.

Kathy Mance, "L.L.Bean President Shares Secrets to Top-Notch Customer Service," *NRF Retail's Big Blog,* September 14, 2010, blog.nrf .com.

Nola Taylor Redd, "Mae Jemison: Astronaut Biography," space.com /17169-mae-jemison-biography.html.

Mae Jemison, *Find Where the Wind Goes: Moments from My Life* (Scholastic Press, 2001).

Story of taxi driver and woman, "A Sweet Lesson on Patience," wimp.com Facebook wall post.

Jo Cofino, "Patagonia Plans Global Campaign for Responsible Capitalism," *The Guardian* UK, February 11, 2013, guardian.co.uk.

CHAPTER 7: Meaning

Shari Caudron, "The Search for Meaning at Work," *Training & Development Journal*, September 1997, Vol. 51, Issue 9: page 24. Available at pathfinderscareerdesign.com/salon/astd.html.

Michael Bergeisen, "Can We Find Happiness at Work?" *Greater Good*, April 1, 2011, greatergood.berkeley.edu/article/item/happiness_at_work.

"Creating Job Satisfaction: Getting the Most from Your Job," October 11, 2011, mindtools.com/pages/article/newCDV_94.htm.

"Wait, Wait, The Moth and Theatre and Mother Theresa," *We Play Different: The Blog @ Boston Court*, January 12, 2012, weplaydifferent.wordpress.com/2012/01/20/2442/.

Gina LaRoche, Facebook wall post, December 16, 2012.

CHAPTER 8: Open Awareness

Elisha Goldstein, PhD, "Mindfulness at Work: An Interview with Mirabai Bush," *Psych Central*, November 1, 2012, blogs.psychcentral.com.

Michael Carroll, "Lead By Achieving Nothing. Seriously," *Forbes.com*, November 16, 2012, forbes.com.

Ryan Grenoble, "Window Washers at Le Bonheur Children's Hospital Wear Spider-Man Costumes for Sick Children," *Huffington Post*, October 22, 2012, huffingtonpost.com.

David Mielach, "'We Can't Solve Problems by Using the Same Kind of Thinking We Used When We Created Them,'" *Business Insider*, April 19, 2012, articles.businessinsider.com.

Winnie Yu, "Workplace Rudeness Has a Ripple Effect," *ScientificAmerican.com*, January 3, 2012, scientificamerican.com/article.cfm?id=ripples-of-rudeness.

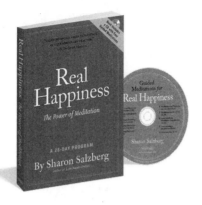

MORE ON MEDITATION

By Sharon Salzberg

"*Real Happiness* is the real deal, a trustworthy how-to, ideal for anyone who wants to cultivate focus, calm, and kindness."

—DANIEL GOLEMAN, author of *Emotional Intelligence*

"*Real Happiness* is a jewel: a beautifully simple, simply beautiful book that can guide and support a newcomer to meditation or enrich and refresh an experienced practitioner. No one could ask for a better teacher."

—MARTHA BECK, columnist for *O* magazine and author of *Finding Your Own North Star*

"An inviting gateway [to] profound well-being and wisdom. With Sharon's gentle voice and exquisite guidance, mindfulness and loving-kindness come to life. . . ."

—JON KABAT-ZINN, author of *Coming to Our Senses* and *Wherever You Go, There You Are*

From one of the world's foremost meditation teachers and spiritual authors, *Real Happiness* is a complete guide to starting meditation and realizing its extraordinary potential to reduce stress, sharpen focus, find inner peace, increase productivity, even protect the brain against aging. It's a 28-day program, and the book includes a CD of Ms. Salzberg's guided meditations.